SAS - 11 Days In A Hell Called Paradise!

**By
Gary Robertson**

SAS - 11 Days In A Hell Called Paradise!
First Edition
Published by DreamStar Books, March 2005
ISBN 1-904166-04-0

Lasyard House
Underhill Street
Bridgnorth
Shropshire
WV16 4BB
Tel: 0870 777 3339
e-mail: info@dreamstarbooks.com

Set in 'Garamond'

Copyright © Gary Robertson

The events and opinions in this book are true and originate from the author.

The moral right of Gary Robertson to be identified as author of this work has been asserted by him in accordance with the Copyright, Designs and Patents Act 1988.

All rights reserved. No part of this publication may be reproduced, stored in a retrieval system or otherwise, except brief extracts for the purpose of review, without the prior permission of the publisher and the copyright owner.

Printed and bound in Great Britain by Antony Rowe Ltd

Acknowledgements

There are many people, too numerous to mention all by name, whom I would like to thank from the bottom of my heart for helping me achieve my goals in life.

My whole family for their support and belief. My friends, acquaintances and enemies – you have all helped me to grow in some way. My martial arts and boxing training partners, in particular my instructors – Rob Kane, Jerry Linskell and Brian & Graham Healy, inspirational and motivational.

The BBC, Eddie Stone and Co. for the experience of a lifetime! Keir and all the 'mountaineering clan' for true comradeship. My friends at the 'Hilltown Horizons Writing Group' – "It's gonna happen!"

Lastly, a huge thank you to Mark Oliver and staff at DreamStar Books for getting this project off its arse!

Massive thanks to you all and cheers to everyone who takes the time to read this story.

About the Author

Born in 1967, Gary Robertson has lived and worked in Dundee all of his life. A factory man and self-confessed fitness fanatic, he also finds time to play the bagpipes in between family life.

His love of writing, in particular poetry, has led him to performing regular live spots locally. He has recently finished writing a play about the Dundee gangs. He is married to Sue and they have two children, Cailean and Eilidh.

For

Sue, Cailean and Eilidh
My inspiration in life.

Mum, Dad and Steff

and

Margaret Macdonald
for showing me what real fighting spirit is.

Foreword

When I was first asked to present SAS "Are you tough enough?" I was not sure what I had let myself in for. I was informed that all of the candidates were exceptionally fit but I knew from experience that that was not the only requirement for someone to pass SAS selection training. So to say the least I was slightly dubious that these people would have what it takes to do a condensed SAS selection. When I first set eyes on the course I was even more dubious as they hardly looked the part, standing there in front of me. The students I am sure, were not aware of what was about to happen to them over the next 10 days or so. After stripping them of all their civilian gear we proceeded to start with the selection. I first became aware of Gary during the first march over Ben Lomond from the north side. Not an easy task. It was his heavy Dundonian accent that drew my attention to him and also his cheerful attitude to each event. Never questioning just getting on with the task given, a very good attitude to have. It was interesting to see how each individual was coping, some did not, and were told to leave, others hanging on by the skin of their teeth, and some finding it not too bad. I was surprised at the mental strength of the women who took part. There were some pretty tough ladies on the course. At each stage the numbers were slowly getting smaller and the tasks were getting harder particularly the mental aspect of the training.

Although the course was only a slight insight into SAS selection, which lasts almost 6 months, it was a very hard 10 days for all the candidates. I would state that it puzzled me at the time and it still does how anyone would voluntarily put him or herself through this particular reality show for no reward. I suppose they were all curious to see how they would fare in their attempt to challenge themselves to the utmost. For that I take my hat off to everyone who took part. But then maybe they are all a little crazy! By the end of the course they were all physically and mentally exhausted.

I have always believed that in any undertaking in life you must have the following three important attributes: mental strength to see the task through, your heart must be in it and finally a little bit of luck. Gary possessed the first two and I'm sure he would be first to acknowledge that he had a little bit of luck along the way, particularly in the swimming pool. I would say without question that the men and women on that first 'tough enough' were all of a better calibre than the subsequent programmes.

Eddie Stone

Introduction

What does your mind conjure up when the simple letters SAS are spread across the media or television? It may be thoughts of men battling against unequal odds, putting their lives on the line and taking their bodies and minds to the absolute limits of their endurance in order to carry out a specific task. The ability to work independently and confidently and also to work with other highly trained men. Men, who could survive come what may.

This formed the basis of my own opinion going on what I had read in various books on the SAS. These people are very special and are only singled out having gone through a rigorous process known simply as 'Selection' which, if you have had the opportunity to read about, you will understand just how tough these guys need to be physically, but probably more important, mentally. There are many different attributes go into the making of a Special Forces soldier and each person applying must search deep inside themselves if they are going to make it through.

Fast approaching 34 years of age, any thoughts of myself being involved in anything to do with the army were a million miles away in my mind. That was until a friend in my work asked if I would be interested in taking part in a new BBC TV series. Reality TV was proving to be very popular amongst the viewing public as candidates threw themselves eagerly at programme producers, hoping for an opportunity of 'fifteen minutes of fame'. Channel 4's Big Brother and ITV's Survivor were taking the nation by storm with large cash prizes being awarded to the eventual winners. Now the BBC had come up with their own concept – a reality series with the intimidating title 'SAS: Are you tough enough?'

They were looking for people who were extremely fit and thought they had what it takes to pass a condensed version of an SAS Selection course. This would be a 'no frills' test of human character, very different to what the other channels were offering.

It was January 2001. As soon as my friend had mentioned the idea, I was already training for it. This was a chance in a lifetime, a dream come true for someone like myself. I'd read the books, now I wanted to take myself on in a proper test of character. There was one small problem. I had to get on the show first!

This is my story.

CHAPTER 1

What If ...?

Working away as usual on the factory line, another New Year had not long past when I found myself asking that post-Celebration question 'What will this year bring?' It had only been a few days since our hillwalking club had been off on its monthly adventure, scaling some of the snow and ice-clad peaks away over in the West of Scotland in a beautiful area called Glen Etive. Conditions had been absolutely perfect for walking and climbing with the big drop in temperatures creating a landscape of frozen beauty. Rivers and waterfalls flowed no more as the prolonged cold snap took a grip. It was an absolutely amazing sight to witness.

We left the factory car park in Dundee as usual on the Friday evening and headed off in high spirits on our merry way, with 'merry' being the appropriate word. Some Friday journeys have turned into full-scale parties with large amounts of alcohol taking the place of common sense and next days' expeditions being worked around thumping hangovers - but that's another story!

We grabbed a few beers in the Kingshouse Hotel near Glencoe and laid plans for the Saturday climb. I say climb because really, in winter, the game is mountaineering and a simple walk can have serious danger attached to it due to conditions. About seven or eight years ago I slipped on a mountain which was in great winter condition and very nearly killed myself due to negligence. I stupidly thought I could get up the hills without using crampons and very nearly paid the ultimate price. Some of the lads do go in for the serious stuff with ropes and jangly bits but they are a different breed altogether. Probably 'nuts' is a better description! Anyway, the banter was flowing as good as the Guinness and some of the old stories were retold for the tenth time but still just as funny. All too soon the drivers had given us the shout and we were on our way to the 'Smiddy', which we'd hired for the weekend. The setting for this club hut is outstanding to say the least. From the front door the view down Loch Etive is stunning and all around massive peaks soar to the sky from the water's edge. Of course, that's when you can see the damn things and they are not covered in mist and cloud and driving rain or snow, but the challenge beckons for everyone who dares to explore them.

Saturday dawned and it was time to get breakfast and a brew on and get the gear together for what was shaping up to be a beautiful morning. The sun blazed over snow-clad peaks as far as the eye could see with a bright blue cloudless sky up above and a fresh, frosty nip in the air, which felt very refreshing as it filled the lungs. Various groups split up for different hills to 'bag' and were rewarded with a cracking day, although the weather did close in later on. You learn to take the good with the bad and enjoy it all the same. Bad weather has never bothered me either in the mountains or when going out for a run, as I love the challenge and hardship it brings. That feeling of rain or sleet being driven into the body by a biting wind is invigorating. Saturday night brought the usual 'crack' with songs, stories, plenty of laughs and a whisky or two to wash it all down. Then there was Sunday morning. A few heads were sore and the liquid being consumed had now turned to water and Irn' Bru. A quick look outside confirmed the dismissal of any thoughts of a venture into the hills. Rain was lashing in at low level, which meant blizzards higher up, and the magnetic lure of a cosy sleeping bag was always going to win 'hands down'. Sorted. I know I said I didn't mind bad weather but sometimes a hangover and a bit of common sense make sound judgement. We were back home for early afternoon and the kids made short work of tiring me out properly. They wouldn't care if I'd just climbed Everest – playing was top of their agenda and quite rightly so.

Right, where was I? Oh yes, the BBC. My mate Cammy, who set up a website for our hillwalking club was passing in the work and stopped for a chat. He asked how the weekender had gone and continued talking for a few minutes more, then casually threw in - 'I've had an email from the BBC asking if anyone would be interested in taking part in a programme about the SAS.' I nearly fell away. He said 'I'll get the email for you later and you can have a look, see what you think.' I was thinking 'Cammy, get it now, get it yesterday, I need to see it.' I was absolutely bursting with excitement but managed to hold out till the next day when he handed me that magic sheet of paper. The gauntlet was thrown down in front of me. 'Are you tough enough? Do you have what it takes to pass SAS selection?'

They were looking for thirty very fit individuals from the public to take part in endurance marches, interrogation, escape and evasion, abseiling and climbing, counter terrorism and more. It was to take place in the month of May over two weeks (in the Brecon Beacons) and was designed so that only one person would complete and win the prize which was to be confirmed later. I couldn't contain my excitement. A chance to have a go at probably the toughest military selection course in the world involving things I would just love doing. I read it and re-read it the whole day wondering what sort of things were going to be in the course, what fitness level would be required, what kind of person would take part. It would have to be some kind of nutter and that nutter couldn't wait for that final bell to ring at three o'clock in order to get home and ring the contact number. My adrenaline was at the overflowing level as I paced back and forth in my bedroom, looking at the phone and wondering what to say. 'Right, here goes.' I phoned Seb Illis at the BBC inquiring about the forthcoming programme which he explained would be very tough, both mentally and physically, describing all the things that were on the email and also the chance if you progressed further, to do a parachute jump. A parachute jump is something I have always wanted to do and had never got around to doing. It just sounded fantastic. I told Seb, 'I've got to be on this programme.' I would have paid to get an opportunity like this.

My application was on its way, and an adventure to beat all adventures. Even before the application arrived, I thought about the training, which might be suited to the task ahead, and the best way to go about it. Usually my training consists of a wide variety of activities ranging from martial arts, boxing, hillwalking, running and fitness work. The hill work could stay. From the books I had already read, initial selection involved some serious tabs (marches) over hilly terrain carrying anything from a fridge freezer up to a small caravan on your back while time was ticking against you. The sparring would have to be knocked on the head for a while. Injuries were something I could do without and they were unavoidable with the training I was doing at the time. Along with my mates Billy, Derek, Craig, Jim and Jerry we'd put on fencing helmets, gloves, a groin protector and sometimes knee pads and proceed to knock the shit out of each other stickfighting. We conjured up these weapons from cut down chimney sweeping brushes, which were made of hard plastic and covered with pipe lagging. These were then taped up tightly and very compact. They did the job perfectly, not enough to kill you but bloody sore enough to let you know you'd been whacked. The idea was to take our training to a more realistic level, although if you took a head shot you acknowledged you would have been finished. We applied the same realistic methods to the grappling training and submission fighting but as I said, injuries were common and trying to run after receiving two dead legs from Thai boxing was near impossible.

Billy and the guys are still training away and the knowledge and friendship I have gained from them is fantastic. I kept up the boxing training just for the sheer intensity, which it offered – a good honest workout. I don't believe there is a harder arena on the planet than the boxing gym and my friend and coach, Brian Healy always drove a Spartan regime, pushing himself to the limits. A great inspiration to myself, and also to all the young lads who turn up to be put through their paces week in, week out. With Brian's brother Graham coaching/training, the guys do a sound job in the boxing gym. Although I wasn't even on the programme, my philosophy from the start was totally geared towards being there, just in case I did get the nod.

The application form arrived within a day or two and was a fairly intense affair, asking all sorts of questions regarding fitness regime, motivation, the hardest thing you've ever done, family thoughts and so on. I tried to answer as enthusiastically as possible, and let the producer know that I wanted to be on the show at all costs. One chance is all you get. Off it went in the post with all my hopes and wishes attached to it. I spoke to my wife Sue, about the possibility of taking part, and she was very supportive, as it would involve me having to take two weeks' holiday from my work. 'Go for it', she said. 'If you want to do it, then do it.' What a gem of a person, and my best friend too! Here was me, if I was accepted, going to take two weeks of family holiday time, and Sue saying 'O.K'. I promised myself, that if I were lucky enough to get on the programme, we would have a wee holiday in October whatever the outcome.

Some days passed before a letter dropped through my letterbox, with a BBC heading on it. Maybe the dream was over. Maybe I had just been getting carried away. When I had first phoned the BBC, I had sort of tongue-in-cheek, sort of serious, said to Sue 'I'll be on that programme,' and now it looked to be happening. The letter informed me that I had made it to the last one hundred contestants and should make my way to London near the end of March to take part in a fitness test. I was over the moon to say the least but kept the lid on it for the time being. Sue was extremely happy for me and kept saying, 'What if?' Even the kids were starting to get a bit excited. I'd mentioned it to a few of the lads in the work and they'd taken great delight in ripping the shit out of me. 'Thanks for the support lads.' The banter in a factory is always top quality and someone's always getting it in the neck. It's no place for the faint hearted at times.

Together with the application, I'd sent a video of myself training, which included Billy and me knocking the hell out of each other with the sticks on a freezing cold February morning in the local park. Some footage running up the Law Hill in Dundee with a 45-pound rucksack was thrown in too. I wondered if the video had helped my cause, imagining a viewing panel to be saying something like, 'We've got to have this headcase on the show!' It seemed a bit better than a plain old photo.

The fitness test was to be a fairly straightforward affair, consisting of a stint on a running machine, a cycling machine and a rowing machine and would last no more than an hour. I have to admit I was very surprised at the choice of exercises and the duration they would last. I thought we would be heaving a small elephant in a rucksack, over the Brecon Beacons for maybe half a day at least. I would have to get on my bike again after ditching it in favour of running and hill work. As far as rowing was concerned, well, three or four times a year at the local pond with my children just wasn't going to get me into the same class as Sir Steve Redgrave. I managed to get a loan of a rowing machine from a mate in the work and packed in a few mini-triathlon sessions into the two or three weeks before the test. March had been a bad month for getting into the hills as the Foot and Mouth crisis took a grip of the country and many outdoor pursuits were knocked on the head for the time being. In Scotland, we faired much better than our neighbours South of the border in England and Wales where the disease had really taken a hold. We had been very lucky in the North, where cases were restricted to the Borders region. It still meant I couldn't go into my beloved hills for now, but by the very end of March, some estates were opening their gates with precautions being taken. I adopted a very selfish view at this point thinking, the more I could visit the mountains here, the more I would have an advantage over contestants from down South, who would have to travel a long way if they wanted to get any hill training in. I kept this thought process going throughout, even though I hadn't been accepted yet. Better to be prepared than not. As the date for the fitness test approached, Sue and I decided to make a weekend of it and stay at my Mum's aunt Cathy and uncle Ted's home in Bushey Heath near Watford. We'd decided to fly down on the Friday night, arriving at Luton airport where Ted was going to pick us up around 11.30p.m. The plan was to have a good chat, catch up on all the news and then jump on the tube in the morning in plenty of time for the fitness test at 2.30p.m. That'll do nicely. Wrong! We were delayed for some time so we grabbed a coffee and settled down with many other passengers to watch the Graham Norton Show which we watch every week. Everyone was chuckling away at the antics, (which can be quite crude at times) and munching away on snacks, when the part of the show where he contacts someone on the Internet smacked everyone in the face. Some people had been trying not to watch, as the content was below the belt at times. They were soon to be blown away as the star of the website proceeded to play 'God Save The Queen' on a penny whistle using only her vagina! It was absolute class. People were fidgeting and trying to ignore it while the rest of us were falling off our seats. It was to get worse when we were moved downstairs ready to board the plane and were delayed further. People naturally gathered round the TV to ease the boredom and were treated to a classic Joan Collins film with plenty of shagging. Cheers Joan, I nearly pissed my pants as people got up (excuse the pun) and walked away uncomfortably to go and read the uninspiring adverts adorning the walls or have a go at counting all the floor tiles in the building. It was the best delay ever!

    The flight was a trifle hairy, as thick mist had descended on the country and made flying conditions quite nasty. The pilot did a fantastic job landing the plane. I don't know how he managed to see the runway in conditions, which nearly had us diverted to Stansted airport. My underpants were starting to go a shade of brown. We finally collected our bags and waited patiently for Ted who had kindly offered to come and collect us. We told him we could grab a taxi but he would hear nothing of it and travelled the thirty-minute journey through dense fog to greet us with a lovely smile. Safely back at home there was much news and stories swapped then it was time to hit the sack. The Grandfather clock chimed like a smaller version of Big Ben. It was 03.00 a.m. I was feeling totally knackered and mentally drained when my head hit the spongy soft pillow but struggled to get to 'slumberland' due to the probable anticipation of tomorrow's events. Ted and Cath gave us a wake up call at 08.00a.m. delivering piping hot tea and biscuits. I was instantly alert, like the times as a child when you have a birthday or other special event and excitement rushes though your body like an express train. Tiredness was instantly forgotten. Breakfast became a battle of wits with Aunt Cath, as more food was offered up to follow the load I'd just managed to shovel in. 'You'll need a good breakfast inside you,' she enthused. My late Gran Bett who was Cath's sister, was exactly the same. Just when you thought you couldn't fit any more grub into an already packed stomach bursting at the seams, Gran would say 'Go on, have another piece of toast, or cake.'

'Thanks Gran but I've already had a half loaf and a good go at relieving Mr. Kipling of some excess in his cake department'. What is it with Grandmothers? They seem to think we are not fed at home and persist in offloading some of their food mountain on to us and won't take 'No' for an answer. Bless them. Love is what they enjoy giving most.

I packed my training gear into the holdall, re-checked it, then Ted ran us to the tube station. Ten minutes later we were on our way to White City in London. I tried to relax but was fighting a constant battle with my inner opponent. 'You're not good enough. What if everyone's better than you? What if you make an ass of yourself?' 'Bring it on' I thought. Negative thoughts have to be destroyed with positive energy and a highly motivated mind. I'd learned a lot from top martial artist and author, Geoff Thompson whose books on fear, stress and positive thinking are a great read for anyone wishing to break out of their comfort zone and dive into various kinds of adversity. We'd arranged to meet Sue's brother Gordon (who'd driven down from Swindon,) outside the BBC buildings. After locating the venue where the test was to be held we decided to go for a cuppa and some dinner in nearby Shepherd's Bush as we had some time to kill. Sue jumped in the front of her brother's little van, leaving me to sprawl in the back over tools, pieces of machinery and other junk, which lay scattered around. Gordon drove like Nigel Mansell, which is par for the course - or race track as it was at this moment in time! No one has a second to spare and road rage seems to simmer near the surface of even the meekest of old grannies. I remember being hunched up in the back as we darted in from one lane to another and spotting a car number plate quite by accident which had the letters SAS at the end of it. I thought to myself 'Maybe it's a sign, today might just be my day.' The thought was gone as quickly as it had entered, there being the more pressing need of holding on for dear life as Gordon hammered on in the merry-go-round that was more like a scene from the 'Wacky Races.' I was thinking sarcastically, 'This is great preparation. A nice relaxing drive through the centre of London with a set of spanners sticking in my kidneys and a large screwdriver trying to skewer me in unmentionable places.' After a bit of dodgy parking we strolled into an upmarket bar with welcoming surroundings and browsed over the menu. I wasn't really in the mood for eating, (especially after Cath's forced feed) with a stomach going like a washing machine on full spin, so I settled for an orange juice and let Sue and Gordon get on with devouring their lunch. The conversation was passing me by as my mind wandered through a maze of thoughts. Sue kept reassuring me, 'Look, you'll be fine. You've done so well getting this far, be proud and give it your best shot.' She was right. There was probably hundreds of people who'd applied and would love to be in the position I was in so I thought 'Yeah. C'mon, let's do it!'

Gordon dropped us off after first, taking us past Wormwood Scrubs, which I'd read about in various books on the Underworld. I thought about the masses of humanity locked up behind those cold intimidating walls, grinding out a hollow existence. We said goodbye to Gordon and headed for the main entrance to the BBC buildings. A terrorist bomb had recently gone off in White City and police messages on billboards were asking for any witnesses to come forward. A crazy thought came into my head. 'What if they were targeting the programme? Surely not.' I dismissed the notion and focused on what lay ahead. People were coming and going, some portraying that 'flushed' look of exertion. Natural instinct has you sizing them up. 'Never mind them. What are you gonna do?' I gave my name to a girl on the desk who met us with a broad smile and a friendly welcome, then walked into the changing facilities to get my gear on. A big Scouser named Jason was getting changed at the same time, so we chatted briefly and exchanged pleasantries then made our way to the sports hall. Contestants were already being put through their paces in groups of ten. Ours would be the last group of the day. Again the mind was checking out strong contenders. The good thing about the programme was that they wanted to see how women would fare in the tough environment of a usually male dominated area. I thought it was a great idea. Equal opportunities and all that! Some of us chatted about our sporting disciplines and interests then it was on to a quick briefing by BBC team members on what was expected.

First up, ten minutes at level 15 on the running machine. Three minutes break. Three minutes of sit-ups, another three-minute break. Ten minutes on the bike, three minutes rest then 2000m on the rowing machine in a time of eight minutes or better. 'Sounds o.k.' I thought. I glanced up at Sue, who was watching from behind the huge windows of the viewing area upstairs. Originally, I was going to London on my own but we then decided to make a weekend of it and right now I felt comforted by her presence. I took on board the 'Good luck' message coming from her lips. Seb Illis from the BBC assured us we weren't racing against each other and that it was as much to do with the content of our application forms as well as performance. So it was looking like a general measure of fitness, plus a small screen test by a BBC crew who were doing interviews while contestants did their stuff.

Ex-SAS man Barry Davies, who'd set the programme up for the BBC and Mike Stroud, who would be the doctor on board were also wandering around assessing. I'd read of Mike's exploits in a couple of his books and also read a couple of Barry's using one in particular as a kind of learning bible. It was an honour to be even under the same roof as these guys let alone be assessed by their watchful gaze.

First up the run, and we're off. If you couldn't hack the pace at level 15 you could bring it down to a more comfortable level but no way was I going to under perform. My lungs felt as though they were on fire through a combination of nerves, adrenaline and only a small warm-up. Getting the muscles and lungs ready before exercise is always very important as it prepares the body to fire on all cylinders and right now I did not feel it. My heart rate and breathing recovered quickly and I began to feel good. The three minute rest was up and we're into the sit-ups with BBC members holding our feet for support and offering some encouragement. Over the years I've always included sit-ups for a strong stomach and this one, which wasn't included in the information sheet, possibly caught some people out. Sixty-five was the required amount during the three minutes, back to the floor then up, a full sit-up, no cheating. I heard others struggling and grunting all around as I pushed in a steady 115. Next up the cycle machines and as hard as you could pedal for ten minutes. Some were strong on this one where as I tried to keep an even pace and save some energy for the final discipline, which was the rowing. I remember being interviewed while on the cycle by a cameraman on various subjects, and trying to sound like I was cruising, while really I was breathing out my arse! He asked as a parting shot, 'Did I think I had what it takes to make it to the end of the course if selected?' 'Yes,' I answered no ifs, buts, or maybes. I needed to be involved in this programme.

Last up, and we're into the rowing. A couple of the guys next to me nearly rowed the machine down the hall and out into the street, they were going so well. I dug in and managed the distance, just inside the eight minutes, but felt I had done well enough and had given it my best shot. The lads all joined in some light-hearted banter when it was over, then everyone went their separate ways to contemplate and await the outcome. Sue came over and gave me a big hug. 'Let's just wait and see,' she said. I told her that three of the guys in my group - Jonathon, Jason, and Geraint would all be on the show, just from hearing of some of their achievements and the strong performances they had pushed in. The likes of the Everest marathon, Iron Man triathlon and other high-endurance events had me listening in awe. I also told Sue that we were probably looking at the winner in Geraint. This guy had won the infamous 'Tough Guy' event and looked totally unruffled by our little training stint. Sue said simply - 'I'm looking at the winner.'

CHAPTER 2

All Systems Go

The days following the fitness test seemed to crawl by at a snail's pace, wondering if the effort had been enough to warrant a place on the programme. Family, friends, and work colleagues asked every day, 'Have you heard yet? Are you gonna be on TV?' I played it all down on the outside but inside, my mind was doing cartwheels. Sometimes I dreamed of getting the call and making it on to national telly then quickly suppressing the thoughts trying not to get carried away. 'Maybe I won't even hear,' I would say to Sue. My two children, Cailean and Eilidh were at it too. 'Daddy, are you going to be on TV, cause if you are, we think you'll win.' Going by the calibre of people I'd seen and spoken to, that statement from my kids seemed like going up Mount Everest doing a handstand, (actually, it's probably been done) but it was a lovely gesture anyway from my two wee angels. I love them to bits. I still trained hard, hoping that if I got the nod I'd at least be prepared, and if things didn't work out I'd revert back to knocking hell out of my mates and vice-versa with some hard sparring.

6th April 2001, Friday morning. The post arrived through the letter box and scattered on the floor. I was on holiday that week and waited eagerly each day for the postman to deliver his goods. 'Make me the happiest man in the world or put me out of my misery.' I searched through the junk mail and letters offering loans or credit cards, the usual crap, which lands on your carpet and sends you racing for the bin. Suddenly, there it was. A letter headed BBC. Adrenaline surged through my body in anticipation. I couldn't wait and ripped at it like a man who'd just received his winning lottery cheque from Camelot for a seven-figure sum. It was worded quite craftily by kicking off with 'Thank you very much for attending ...blah ...blah.' I waited for the knife through the heart but it never came. Instead the next paragraph started, 'We are delighted to inform you that you have been chosen...' 'Fuckin' yahoo!' I was reading it to Sue, who was quite ingloriously sitting on the loo at the time. I had paused after the first paragraph thinking 'Well that's that over.' Next thing, BANG, we're jigging in the toilet (after Sue had quickly hauled her knickers up) trying to take in the sentence I had just read out. I think Sue was more excited than me, which was some going considering I had just opened a letter better than anything Camelot could throw at me. People may not believe a statement like that but I can honestly say, Santa Claus had just delivered the best present ever as far as I was concerned.

Then it hit me. The negative thoughts that creep up on you, catching you unawares and try to drag you down in a whirlpool of self-doubt. 'What if you're off first? You'll be a laughing stock. You can't go on TV, they'll never understand your funny East of Scotland accent.'

'Well bollocks.' I'd done the self-doubt and low self-esteem bit all through my young life and no way was I bottling something like this. Its you against you when it comes to making decisions in life, not the journey or the task which lies ahead, but you. Inside your mind, in the red corner, Mr. Negative stands there scowling, stalking, preying, waiting to pounce on any weakness, which shows itself. In the blue corner, Mr. Positive stands, staring ahead, confident, ready to take on come what may, but quite often finds himself overcome by a wave of anxiety and fear, and ultimately, destruction as Mr. Negative delivers his knockout blow. Many people find Mr. Negative a formidable and sometimes unbeatable adversary (I was one) preferring to live life in the safety of a comfort zone. If you can find courage and strength from inside, and feed off inspiration from others, Mr. Negative's arse can be well and truly booted into touch until the next confrontation, because he never really leaves you. Always looking for a way back in. Take adversity on and life can be a joy to live. Your only limitations are the ones you create yourself.

I smashed the thoughts from my head, which were threatening to spoil the biggest event in my life outside of getting married to Sue, and giving birth to two incredible bundles of love. And anyhow, if people didn't know what the hell I was saying on TV, Ceefax would help them out with subtitles!

Sue started ringing family and friends, relaying the news that I had been picked to appear on the programme, while I wandered around the house in a daze. It took some sinking in. 'Right Sue, I'm gonna have to 'up the training' a bit more with plenty visits to the hills.' I half pleaded, half laid it on the line. She jokingly said 'That'll be bloody right' or that's the way I interpreted it, but she knew deep down how much this meant to me and gave me an unlimited 'license to roam' pass. I felt pretty confident that come May, other contestants would not have been able to get much mountain training in due to the 'Foot and Mouth' restrictions. I hoped that the training I had put in so far would stand me in good stead, having gone through some testing Scottish winter conditions. Also, it would be a great way to make another dent in the Munro's (hills over 3,000 feet) which I was steadily whittling down. 284 in all, and a smashing challenge to set yourself, doing them as fast as you like or taking a lifetime of visits in all weathers to 'bag' them as the saying goes. I was sitting around the 240 mark, stretching back over ten years of escapades with the lads, many of whom had already completed them or were nearing the final summit. I would say though that the pub round had been slightly harder and a more serious undertaking than the hills!

Working three shifts in a factory had never been a problem training-wise but sometimes when you're overdoing it a bit, you find yourself nodding off at break times with a general run-down feeling. Some days I'd put in three sessions. Maybe getting up at 5 o'clock in the morning on an early shift to run four or five miles, have a shower and then it was off to work. A two or three mile run during dinner-break and home at 3.30pm to play with the kids. After they'd gone to bed, a session of circuit training for an hour would usually see me going to bed far too late and getting around five and a half to six hours sleep, ready for the next day's onslaught. Varying your training is the key to not getting bored, plus alternating hard days with less intense days. Rest is another major factor, but something I find quite difficult to do, feeling like you're cheating having a day or two off, although it's got to be done. Nightshift can be funny sometimes when heading out for a run at three in the morning on your break, and lorry drivers pass you thinking, 'Bloody hell, he's keen!' Or down at the local beach at eight o'clock in the morning, doing sprints in the sand with a luminous green punchbag weighing 60 pounds on your shoulder, and people opening their curtains thinking, 'What the hell…?'

Foot and mouth was by now, widespread throughout much of England and Wales, but only touched on Scotland in the Borders area so far. It meant most rural areas up north were still accessible with precautions, but outdoor activities in the south were decimated. There was a real worry now that the programme would not go ahead or would be rescheduled to a later date.

The inevitable happened and I must admit I was devastated. The phone rang and the news I had been dreading was duly delivered. The Brecon Beacons, a mountainous region in South of Wales (where filming was to take place), had closed its boundaries to the public. 'Shit, and double shit' I thought as I put the phone down. I'd been studying those maps, solid. Training had been building up nicely and the body, hopefully, was ready to peak. Looking back now, the move from May to late August was a Godsend. I can honestly say, the one area I lacked in and kind of neglected was to play a major part in my progress on the 'selection'. Swimming. I've always enjoyed a bit of swimming but usually it consisted of one session a year on the annual holiday or lately, since the kids came along, a play in the local pool. Somehow, shooting down the flumes and doing summersaults and belly flops on the diving boards were not part of SAS training in the manuals. The story in the pool will unfold later.

I took a step back from training, rested three or four days and allowed myself a 'night out', then set my sights on a new date and building up the training again. I had hoped if the show went ahead in May, the weather would be crap, and navigating might be tricky for contestants who may not have visited the hills too often possibly giving myself a small advantage, although I have been 'temporarily misplaced' in the hills on occasion. That's the technical term for 'Where the hell am I?' Marches over the hills are a big part of initial Selection so I concentrated on getting in the miles, filling the rucksack with weights and extra gear, having anything from 40 pounds up to 70 pounds. It was quite funny on some weekenders with the lads when I'd struggle to get my pack from the boot of the car, and that lot were putting little bumbags on to their backs. 'Come on ya big jessie,' would filter down to my ears from above, through swirling mist and driving rain as the lads set a mean pace. 'Yeah, this is where it's at' I thought. 'When the going gets tough…crack on.' A good laugh is a must and we always had that in abundance. One weekend we decided to 'bivvy out' in the Cairngorms, sleeping in waterproof Gore-tex bivvy bags and taking in some of the 4000-foot mountains on the way. The lads headed up to the Linn o' Dee car park near Braemar and planned to walk in the three miles to an area near Derry Lodge where they could get their heads down in a comfy spot. Finishing a backshift at 11.00 pm on the Friday night I planned to meet up with them which I realised later, would be like finding a needle in a haystack in the pitch black. They told me if the weather was bad they'd be in Bob Scott's bothy. Bothies are usually old derelict houses, sometimes in the middle of nowhere, which the MBA (Mountain Bothy Association) renovate and make liveable through work parties and volunteers, making a superb 'hotel' in isolation. Most have a fireplace and dead wood can be gathered, or coal or peat carried in to create an atmosphere at night where anyone can gather round after a good day in the hills to tell stories, sing songs, have a whisky or three and a damn good 'crack'. The bothy culture, is a culture all on its own, and many varied characters pass through their doors.

It was mid June (which does not mean a lot in Scotland) and we were hoping for a nice weekend of blistering hot sunshine and cool summer breezes. As soon as I stepped out of the car at 12.40am, someone pressed the switch on and the rain came down in torrents, with a strong gale blowing in the face. I zipped up my waterproof jacket, switched on my headtorch, and marched off into the forest with a 60-pound pack on my back. Walking alone can be eerie sometimes, especially at night, and mind games roll around in your head, questioning every sound and movement you've heard or seen. At Derry Lodge I found no sign of my mates so I spent some time searching for the bothy which the 'softies' would be in. After a fruitless search (some navigator!) I looked for a comfortable spot to set up home. Even if I'd found the bothy I'd made up my mind I was sleeping out tonight. I suppose I was on a kind of toughening up crusade. Under a huge pine tree I managed to locate a piece of ground, which was only half-sodden. This would be my bivvy. I worked quickly, changing into dry clothes then set out my mat and bivvy bag and snuggled in for the night. The time was 02.15am and rain drummed on the waterproof material in a constant, monotonous beat. I pulled all the material in to leave a small hole to breathe out off and closed my eyes, trying to relax but my mind just wouldn't relax, no matter how tired I was feeling. A fierce wind kept crashing through the trees, making branches and trunks creak under the strain. 'What the fuck was that? There's got to be someone or something there.' My mind was playing games (which I was in no mood for) as every sound was questioned by my hypersensitive state.

I remember having really strange and abstract dreams when I did eventually doze off that night - dreams which seemed so real. I think in a situation when you are all alone in the outdoors subconscious thoughts are thrown into the mind's cauldron creating some pretty weird visions.

There's a comforting feeling in the morning when your eyes crack open, witnessing a new day being born, and getting a clear picture of just where the hell you are. It was 7.05am and within minutes I had a brew on and some scoff down my neck. Ten minutes later the lads wandered around from behind a small hill and we then realised that we had been sleeping in close proximity to each other. We all had a right laugh. As the wind and rain had died away and a brighter scene developed, the midges decided to rear their ugly heads, hastening our departure and sending us on our way into the heart of the Cairngorms. A big day was on the cards, taking in Devil's Point, Sgor an Lochan Uaine, Cairn Toul, Braeriach and Ben Macdui. The rest of the lads climbed this final one before descending to the 'Hutchison Memorial Hut.' I had to be home Saturday night, so said 'cheerio' after Braeriach and marched with as hard a pace as I could muster down the final ten miles of the Lairig Ghru to the car park. It was a big day involving around some five thousand feet of climbing and twenty-odd miles. My feet and shoulders seconded that.

I've tried to let you, the reader, in on the special atmosphere, which goes with hillwalking or mountaineering, a pastime, which really does enhance character building. A stiff battle with the elements is a sure way of re-charging the mental batteries. Supplementing this I did loads of circuit training, various kinds of running (sometimes with a 40-pound pack on) boxing training and this I hoped would see me through, all the while thinking 'OK the others are gonna be pushing it, I'll push some more then.' Oh yeah, and I threw in a few more visits to the swimming pool, doing what I thought were some decent sessions. As the end of August loomed, adrenaline started circulating round my body, each day bringing bigger surges. I had managed to steer clear of serious injury with just a few niggling problems, which most people who lead sporting lives can be prone to. A recurring knee strain, a pulled groin, and two corns on my right foot, were the battle scars I was carrying, but nothing to worry about. One thing I had noticed throughout the year was the frequency I was getting chesty colds, usually a sign of overtraining. It's a vicious circle, you either train or you rest. Getting the balance is the tricky part, although two amputated legs would not have stopped me going!

CHAPTER 3

Day 1

Into The Unknown

The three happy, smiling faces disappeared out of view as the train pulled away from Dundee station - No contact with the three most important people in my life for eleven days. My wife Sue, Cailean, and Eilidh would be my strength for the massive challenge ahead, which I was hoping, would be the whole duration. The BBC had posted train tickets, which would take me to Stirling, only about an hour from my home, then I would be taken to the programme's location. I had worked out from snippets of information beforehand that it was going to take place in Scotland, but where? As mentioned before, Foot and Mouth had put a stop to the Brecon Beacons. A chance read of a Scottish Sunday paper gave me a clearer picture when they did a small article about the programme, saying filming was about to take place at a secret location between Aberfoyle and Callander. Actually, they got it wrong, but not by much.

So here I was sitting on my holdall, on a very busy train, with a million thoughts racing through my brain. The 'Good Luck' messages from family and friends had been taken on board, now it was time to get down to business. 'Just don't be first home' I thought. My plan all along was to take it one day at a time and see where it got me, every new day being a bonus and also a fresh challenge. My holdall was like a sofa, it was so big. It must have weighed around 60 pounds and was full of very important kit, which I had checked meticulously, leaving nothing to chance. Basically, it consisted of two pairs of Karrimor KSB boots, an old pair and a newer pair, the latter being slightly heavier in weight, three base layer thermal tops, two fleece tops and two pairs of trackster bottoms. I had a Gore-tex jacket and trousers, two hats, a pair of gloves, compass, medical kit, survival kit, headtorch, eight pairs of socks, ten pairs of undies, thirty Mars Bars, eleven tins of Red Bull, other items of food and various bits and pieces. I'd even thrown in plastic bags for crapping in, which I'd read about! Guess what? They took the bloody lot from us! We'll get to that shortly.

On the train I looked at other people going about their daily business, wondering what was filling their minds. I don't think it was the same as the stuff that was churning through my mind. As we neared Stirling station the adrenaline was showing 'full' on the meter, a real surge of fear, apprehension, and excitement, all mixed in one crazy concoction. I walked, well sort of staggered to the main entrance with this bloody great 'treasure chest' slung over my shoulder, expecting at any moment to see the BBC representatives and camera crew. Nothing! 'O.K. it must be a set up. The cameras will be on you from a distance, seeing how you cope with this unexpected development.' Twenty minutes passed by and I decided I had better phone home to get a contact number. Eventually a message came over the tannoy system at the station for me to make my way to the main desk. The BBC said there had been a bit of a mix up and I was told to grab a taxi to the Kinlochard Hotel, where someone would meet me to pick up the 'tab'. Fifty minutes had passed and all sorts of nonsense had gone through my head. I'd even thought about getting a taxi to Callander and searching for the location, but it's a good job I didn't, as I would have still been there yet, looking for it. We pulled up at what was a fairly big, plush hotel set in magnificent surroundings, complemented today by the fantastic weather. I entered a large dining area to find most contestants already there and tucking into some scoff. It's funny how you feel the eyes of others locking on to you especially when the room is full of highly competitive people. I did likewise and scanned the faces at the dinner tables, checking out my rivals.

I gave my name to someone then grabbed a plateful from the buffet (little did we know, this would be the last real food for a while) and joined a few others at a table. Adrenaline started tracking through my body while on the outside I tried to look calm and relaxed. I quickly noticed the seemingly high proportion of contestants from around the London area and how they instantly bonded with one another. I don't know if it's a Scottish trait or not but personally I preferred to keep myself to myself for the time being, generally sussing the whole scene out first. A quick nod and a 'hello' was passed between myself and the seven other guys at the table then I settled down to fill my rumbling stomach. I glanced over to the guy sitting across from me and thought to myself, 'He's definitely a boxer.' The flat nose is usually a dead giveaway. The guy smiled and we exchanged a few words. This was Del Boy - a character whom I would find later to be a warrior with a hugely compassionate heart. With the ice now broken, the others spoke and had a laugh when I told them I had only to travel a fairly short distance to get here today. Most of them had flown into Edinburgh and for some this was to be their first visit to Scotland. What a baptism of fire it would be! I noticed Jason and Jonathon (two of the guys from the fitness test) were at another table and gave them a nod. After looking around the hall I realised Geraint, the guy who impressed us at that same fitness test, was not here.

'We can't be staying here, this is far too soft', I wondered, taking in the array of comforts set before us. Each of us had to go upstairs to a room where we were interviewed on a whole host of questions, ranging from motivation, thoughts on the programme, to how far you thought you could go. Waiting your turn in the corridor was like waiting to go into the dentist for a tooth extraction then sitting your driving test straight after. It was a very nerve-wracking experience to have for the first time, the camera focused on you and two guys from the BBC grilled you. Apart from that, the heat in the small room made any thoughts of trying to look cool, impossible.

Afterwards I strolled around the grounds outside, soaking up the sunshine and had my first chat with Karl, a soft-spoken and well-mannered man who harnessed a fierce inner competitive streak. He hailed from Derbyshire and worked for Her Majesty's government as a police officer. We were both about the same build and height but I remember thinking, 'This guy looks the business.' Karl informed me among other things, that he did fell-running. I knew these guys could motor and Karl proved himself later in the hills as he blew the opposition away, leaving us trailing in his wake. As I tried to relax and absorb the idyllic scene around me, I felt a piece of paper in my pocket and took it out. It was a note from Sue telling me to do my best and no matter what the outcome was I would always be a winner in her eyes. It made me quite emotional. Luckily there were no other contestants around as they would have written me off as a big Scottish jessie and quite rightly so! My alibi was set just in case another contestant witnessed my tears. 'No honest, I'm okay, it's just severe hay fever.' Time passed slowly as we all realised, 'This is it, showtime, no turning back.' Mike Stroud floated around the company, chatting with everyone and getting to know people's backgrounds. Most of us were interested in hearing of his many exploits around the world, with particular attention being focused on his crossing of the Antarctica with Ranulph Fiennes, pulling sledges which weighed something in the region of 500 pounds each. Totally inspiring, and getting to meet him in the flesh was a great highlight for myself. We seemed to be hanging around for ages in the Hotel and it was during this time that I got speaking to some of the other contestants. I quickly became aware that there was going to be some tough competitors out there, a real mix of triathletes, marathon runners, rugby players and various other disciplines - Some serious athletes with a strong will to succeed.

Gary Hunter from the production team introduced himself and gave us all a briefing saying that an army truck would be arriving shortly to take us to the camp, which was about ten to fifteen minutes away. The excitement grew as we gathered in the car park and one by one were called onto the truck. Space was at a premium as we crammed into the back along with all our kit. Some of us sat in anticipated silence while others were cracking jokes and having some fun during the drive to Drumlean Farm, which would be our adopted home for the days ahead - hopefully till the end. The truck halted near the entrance to the camp and awaited the signal to enter. Another lengthy delay prolonged the mentally sapping process. Everyone just wanted to get out of the truck and get on with it. One contestant kept peeking through the canvas and proceeded to give us a running commentary of the camp set-up in a very annoying broad Yorkshire accent. I had the over-powering urge to tell him to 'shut it' but thought better of it. Not a good start I reasoned.

Any laughter soon died away fast as the tailgate dropped down and voices shouted at us to get our arses off the truck, pronto! We came face to face with the SAS for the first time. Four figures dressed all in black harangued us constantly to move quicker. Bodies stumbled from the truck, tripping over baggage and quietly cursing as the vocal onslaught continued. It was at this moment I thought about these mysterious guys, the shadowy characters from a regiment much has been written of, but only they know the real truth. I allowed myself a little smile at the 'privilege' of seeing their faces – faces that Joe Public never sees.

Darkness was creeping in as a helicopter hovered around the sky, spraying a beam of light on the scene as if hunting some fugitive. Bright spotlights situated around the camp dazzled our eyes. The whole scene seemed very intimidating but at the same time was also very impressive, with two towers decked in camouflage, a perimeter fence, six canvas tents for competitors, and four bigger tents for staff and camera crew. The latter were used only as working centres and not for accommodation. The television crew and SAS would be 'roughing' it in the hotel – perks of the job!

A right ramshackle bunch assembled before the company. I think it would be fair to say that every soul standing there had a heart that was racing furiously. This would be a totally different ball game from competing in say a marathon, or a major endurance event. Fear of the unknown was everything. As we stood there waiting it all reminded me of the TV programme from years ago about a Japanese prisoner of war camp called 'Tenko'. Thankfully we were not in that situation. It was worse! We couldn't even line up straight and were told so from a man with a rough Scottish accent standing a few feet in front of us. Enter Eddie Stone, a typical Sergeant Major-type with an unsmiling look of hardness and a body compact and solid. The crew-cut hairstyle and tattoos added to the menacing appearance. Some individuals seem to generate an aura around themselves and this was certainly one of these people. I had never met the guy in my life but straight away you could feel a power of some kind. He stood in front of us like a lion stalking his prey. Eddie, ex-SAS, was our Staff Sergeant but would be addressed as 'Staff'. Four SAS men stood in the rear, the DS (directing staff). 'Fuck eyeballing them, I'll just stare straight ahead.'

There was no wind and the midges were treated to a three-course meal from us all. If you have never sampled the Scottish midge, especially the West Coast breed, I would recommend it at least once in your life. The Japanese game show 'Endurance' could have included the terrible little insects in their programme, maybe having contestants stand bollock-naked on a calm, damp day, in the middle of a field for as long as possible. They'd be lucky if they'd have managed ten seconds!

Eddie stood there with just a t-shirt on (and trousers and boots of course) while members of the film crew covered themselves from head to toe in a vain bid to protect themselves from the squadrons of minute vampires. I was well impressed.

He started, 'You have come here to see if you're tough enough and have what it takes to join the SAS. Most of you won't make it - maybe none of you will. You will be pushed harder, faster, and for longer than you have ever done in your lives. If you want to leave now, get back on the truck.' As he called out everyone's name, it became apparent that one volunteer had not bothered to turn up. Maybe he or she knew what was in store for us. I think everyone must have realised at that point that it was going to be extremely hard. He added, 'Let's get you looking like soldiers. Strip down to your underpants, get a base layer top, a hat, socks and gloves and bin the rest. Everything you need will be in your bergen (rucksack) and a set of army clothes will be issued, as well as an SLR rifle (deactivated).'

It was just as well that we were allowed to keep our undies on, as the midges would definitely have had my wedding tackle stripped down like a shoal of piranhas. I couldn't believe they were taking all of my precious gear. Oh well, at least we were all in the same boat.

One of the DS had us gather around him and showed us how to strip and re-assemble an AK47 rifle then we were given a number and told which tent to go to. It was tent 2 for me, and four other people to get acquainted with. The tents were the old style canvas ones with a distinct musty smell to them and simple door flaps that tied shut with string. First priority though was to get our heads together and assemble the army beds. From our bergens we held the little Mag-light torches we had been supplied with in our teeth thus freeing our hands to get on with the task. It was like putting together those complicated kitchen units from a DIY store. We mucked in together and got there in the end. Introductions were brief as we were all in need of some serious sleep. A short character round-up of my tent buddies went as follows: Rosie, was a chatty, friendly kind of lass. I don't know where the hell she came from or what she did fitness-wise, but I'll never forget what she did for us after the 'Long Drag' march. Dave Mann at forty-seven, was the oldest contestant on the programme but an extremely fit chap still winning marathons and the like. Lee, a big strongly built muscular lad struck me as a very determined character. He was here to win. Nic I found to be an unconscious comedian and a top 'soft boy' after sneaking his whole cleaning kit into the tent. I'm sure he had deodorant, hairspray, aftershave, body lotion the lot. I thought to myself, 'You won't last a minute here' but how wrong could I have been.

Ominously, situated up near the roof of the tent, was a small camera, which could mean only one thing. We'd be getting up at the crack of dawn and be filmed in a state of panic and confusion. I tried to relax as I lay on my camp bed but my heart was still pounding too quickly for my own liking. The time was around 11.00 pm and although we had not done anything so far, it had been a fairly stressful day. I was tired but couldn't force myself to sleep; always a problem when you know you'll be up early. I kept going over the strip down and re-assembly of the AK47 in my head in between counting sheep.

CHAPTER 4

Day 2

Bergen Time

It must have been around 03.00 am when what sounded like an atomic bomb going off in my ears, entered the doorway of the tent. 'Get your fucking arses out of there on the double. You've got two minutes!' The DS were screaming as they moved from tent to tent. It's a funny feeling when you think you have everything organised the night before, and realise it all goes to shit when five of you wake up at the same time, trying to get ready in a space no bigger than a small shed. I will never forget that morning for as long as I live. Most of the others were lined up as tent 2 received a further bollocking. 'Fucking move it in tent 2.' I'm sure I was still sleeping when I ran onto parade, but soon come to when the bright spotlights hit my eyes. The cold, fresh morning air (more like night air) didn't take long to alert everyone's senses. Eddie gave us a tongue-lashing for not being ready quick enough and for turning out in a bit of a state. We were given thirty minutes, which rapidly turned into twenty-five, to get some breakfast down our necks and be back on parade. I watched, as many opened their ration packs and began to cook a breakfast or brew up a cuppa on their hexi-burners. 'Bad move' I thought as I nibbled away on some snacks. We may have had time for a brew, but cooking seemed to be cutting it a bit fine, plus you would need to wash your kit. Time up and we're back on parade, with one or two cookers still burning away. The DS were on to it straight away. 'Whose lovely little breakfast is this?' asked Eddie. A mess tin full of porridge was sitting cooking itself by one of the tent entrances. One of the girls owned up and was given a bollocking and told to empty the contents and get it back in her pack. Lesson learned. Already we were learning the punishment for reckless behaviour, dropping a rifle or general untidiness when ten or twenty push-ups were meted out to the offenders. The rifle had to be no further than an arm's length at any given time, even if you needed the toilet. Many times at first, we'd forget it and pay the price in push-ups, or if you were lucky someone would remind you discreetly that you'd left it. I suppose it makes good sense to condition the mind as a silly thing like leaving a weapon misplaced in a war situation could cost a soldier his or her life.

'Sorry to disturb your beauty sleep but you're going on a little march called Point to Point,' hissed Eddie sarcastically. Our Bergens were made up to 35lbs with the help of two house bricks, then we boarded the wagon to head for our first bout with the hills. We hadn't even got out of the camp when the truck keeled over and stuck in a drainage ditch, sitting at what seemed like a very precarious angle. It was well and truly stuck. We gingerly extracted ourselves in an orderly fashion, as the feeling was that 'this thing might just tip.' People stood around bewildered as the DS decided on the next course of action. 'What a fine start this is,' I thought. Eventually a couple of Land Rovers arrived on the scene and luckily I was in the first group to be taken to our start point. As the vehicle trundled along a rough track my eyes and mind worked overtime for any clues as to where we were heading. We pulled up at a remote farm and were ordered out. It was a case of playing a waiting game as the Land Rovers journeyed back and forth to camp ferrying all the volunteers. I don't know if it was a build up of nerves or just the plain fact that I was bursting for a crap but I was in a desperate emergency situation. Thankfully I had a little time on my hands while the vehicles went on their last journey. To people who are not the outdoor type, the question they ask of 'Where do you go for the toilet?' is always an amusing one. Some seem visibly impressed when sarcastically answered, 'Yeah, I just run ten miles from the mountain top to the nearest public lavatory and do the business there.' Realistically, as was my dilemma at this moment in time, I took off hotfoot (with my rifle of course) and disappeared behind the cover of some fern plants. These also had to double up as toilet paper and it was a peculiar-walking soldier who returned to the company.

When all of us were finally gathered we were given the first RV (or grid reference), which went straight to the top of the mountain directly behind us. It was Ben Lomond. Although I had climbed it before on my hill travels the view facing me now was sheer rugged beauty as the first rays of morning sun washed over the high ridgelines. This was well off the beaten track of the conventional route up to the top. I think the idea for this particular march was to recreate the famous 'Fan Dance' in the Brecon

Beacons, which means around 24 or 25 km distance and three times up and down the mountain. I had been studying the map for the Brecons extensively and on comparing the two routes together, Ben Lomond definitely had more climbing involved. We'd heard rumours from a certain source that we had plenty of time to complete the task, and to let the 'fliers' take off if they wanted to. As far as staying on the programme was concerned, you were looking to finish in the leading group but as far as equalling SAS times for the 'Fan', well argument could be made concerning height difference, terrain, and so on. A lovely morning was shaping up as we left the farmyard and headed for the ridgeline, backed by a cracking blue sky. The late summer colours on the fiery hillside were comfort and sanctuary for the mind's eye as the pain of burning thigh muscles and screaming lungs kicked in. The time was around 07.00 am and it felt great to be alive. A couple of hundred metres uphill we were met with the challenge of helping to dig out a little rough terrain vehicle, which was stuck in a peat bog. I'm sure it was a set-up, just to see if everyone would muck in to lend a hand. 'Expect the unexpected' to the point of near paranoia. I kept repeating the mantra in my head. Onwards and upwards we went. The more height we gained, the more the field spread out with some contestants lagging well behind even at this early stage. I was also quite shocked to find the amount of contestants who were not proficient in the use of a map and compass. Incredibly, one person had actually asked me to give them a crash coarse in map-reading while I browsed at an Ordnance Survey map in the hotel foyer the previous day!

Some were walking in groups, which was fine for a friendly stroll in the hills, but on a proper Selection it would have been a big no-no. I couldn't help thinking that if we'd had some of our usual Scottish mountain weather, there may have been bodies wandering off to Fort William or Berwick-upon-Tweed, but today it was kind. As I approached the summit, a small group was already huddled around the stone cairn. There was no one there to give us the next grid reference so I descended a little to get out of the wind and quickly pulled on my waterproof clothing and grabbed a quick piece of chocolate. The wind was howling and mist swirled around, while showers of rain swept over us. 'Where the hell did the nice weather go to?' This was 'home' to me but I couldn't help thinking how some of the other contestants were feeling in this alien environment. A number of them had never set foot on a hill before. If I was brutally honest, this is exactly the conditions I (and probably the DS) had hoped for – cold, uncomfortable teeth-gritting weather.

Through the mist, the shadowy figure of one of the DS appeared and gave us our next destination. By now, a large contingent of the starting twenty-nine had gathered but it wasn't long before the field became strung out again. It felt good to be moving as the delay had caused our bodies to chill and muscles to stiffen. Once we dropped down a few hundred metres the dense cloud was beginning to dissipate and it was just about possible to make out the general area of the RV away in the distance. As this route went well off the beaten track, any hopes of a path were non-existent and the going got considerably harder. Deep heather, muddy pools and numerous tussocks hampered fast progress and made everyone tread cautiously. Fear of spraining an ankle or twisting a knee kept you constantly on alert. The 35lbs on my back still felt comfortable enough although the two house-bricks inside the bergen were a pain in the arse. I'd placed them in the top of the pack to keep the weight 'high' but the downside was that any time you went in for food or clothing these bloody things would be in your way! The secret was to put all the snack-type food along with the water bottle into your belt-kit thus cutting down on wasted stoppage time. I felt I was going well enough at this point, not pushing it too hard. My water bottle was re-filled at the checkpoint and my pack was weighed to see if I'd chucked any of my precious 'stones.' Eddie asked if I'd like to 'bin it' (quit). 'No Staff,' I answered forcefully. Next grid reference - Back over the rough ground from where we'd just come and straight up Ben Lomond again. It seemed a long way off. 'Okay, just get on with it.' I was constantly talking to myself. Focus the mind, then it was on through the squelching, boggy expanse once more. For any of the others not used to the mountains, this idea of heading right back to where we'd just been must have felt rather soul-destroying. When walking on your own, a thousand thoughts run through your head. You've got to make sure any negative ones are pushed well away. Wee songs and silly ditty's seem to do the trick. Twinges of cramp threatened my legs as I approached the final steep ascent. The familiar whirr of a helicopter's rotor blades drew nearer and nearer until just a stone's throw above, the machine hovered and readied for touchdown. The noise and force of the down-draught was immense. Three figures jumped out from the cockpit and moved quickly away as the helicopter lifted gracefully upwards before shortly disappearing behind the hillside.

They were Graham Cooper, the programme's producer, Dermot O' Leary, the show's host and Gary, one of the medical team. Graham commented to me that we might be going for it (Ben Lomond) a third time. I wondered if this was just a psychological diversion, another little ploy to gnaw away at contestant's resolve. 'Bring it on' I replied. If they'd said ten times, then ten times it would have to be! The sun broke out again on top giving a fantastic panoramic view. I'd already done this mountain in winter, being one of the Munro's, so today there was no time for idly dwelling on scenery. We were all involved in a personal war with our bodies and minds.

On arrival at the cairn one of the DS asked me, 'How many towers in the camp?' 'Four, I think staff.' 'Oh are there?' he questioned, rather sarcastically. I found out later there were only two. Bad observation. Next, he hit me with, 'What are the names of the others in your tent?' 'Oh fuck, ehm… Lee… ehm… Nic….' 'Right, go and sit over there, no talking, the DS will call for you!' I was rather annoyed with my mental performance but drew some comfort from a square of chocolate and a dry, tasteless biscuit. A few minutes later the call came, along with last night's AK47. 'Strip it and put it back together.' I think I did fairly well here, probably due to the lack of sleep from the previous night, going over and over it in my head. A few hillwalkers passed as I left the summit for the second time that day and surveyed the route down to our original start point at the farm. These members of the public must have wondered what all the activity was for on what would usually be a quiet Monday lunchtime. I overtook a few of the others on the way down and knew there were still many behind. Time to take the foot off the gas for a bit. One of the lads caught up with me and started chatting as we slipped, tripped and stumbled our way down. It was Matt - a big powerhouse of a man. His trade was mountain guiding in the Alps so our little 'wander' today posed no problems for a guy of his calibre. Strangely enough, Matt was the only contestant on the programme who smoked but if this was a handicap then hell, it never showed! I instantly struck up a rapport with him but was also mindful of his potential to do well in our Selection. He was another whom I placed near the top of the pecking order in terms of strong candidates (even at this early stage) but there was a long, hard path to follow in the meantime. A couple of hundred metres from the farm we split, being conscious of walking in company. I gave my number to the DS and half expected to be given the grid reference for the Ben Lomond summit again but it never came. Was I relieved? Most definitely but like I said, if we had to go then you just crack on and get the job done. From start point to finish we were never given the full route and ultimately for some this proved to be their undoing. When I turned into the farmyard there were already four or five contestants resting near a barn and comforting themselves and their weary feet. Among them was Karl who had flown over the route and 'clocked in' first. I chose a spot a little away from the others and removed the bergen from my shoulders then set about getting a brew on. With the others already cooking, the smell of food hit me like a two hundred pound anvil in the head! It was time to replace the lost calories of over-exertion and under-eating. The Arctic ration packs we were told, contained six thousand calories but they certainly didn't feel like it on the stomach. Indeed, as the days went on most of us developed a craving for fatty foods, and even the most serious athletes amongst us were dreaming of a Big Mac or some chip shop cuisine. News was reaching us of some contestants getting disorientated and wandering off in the wrong direction while others were injured or simply way too far back and outside of the time limit. I was surprised to see big Jason sitting in one of the Land Rovers in the farmyard. He seemed to be in a lot of pain from an injury which had been dogging him in his build-up training. I thought the big Scouser would be there or thereabouts at the end of all this, but now it was all over for him. I could only sympathize with him and imagine how he must have been feeling. Personally I would have been utterly dejected. I took great encouragement from a few words he passed on to me before we parted. 'You go and do well in this,' he said. 'What a nice touch' I thought, especially as it was coming from someone whom I believed would be involved in the final outcome of this whole course. One by one stragglers wandered wearily into the farmyard with a few not even having time for a hot meal. Those of us who had arrived earlier were afforded the luxury of re-fuelling our bodies and stealing some shut-eye. To say it would be needed would be a massive understatement. We were taken back to camp in the late afternoon sunshine and told to get a bite to eat and some rest. It was great just to get the boots off and chill out for a while but for some this meant only anguish - feet were starting to tear up already. Later we were called onto parade where Staff Sergeant Eddie Stone announced the first dismissals. From the twenty-nine who originally started, there seemed like a hell of a lot of names being shouted out, decimating our numbers in one fell swoop. 'Fine' I thought, 'I'm not going home first which is a bonus.' The guys' back home would have torn me to shreds!

As those of us who were left contemplated getting our heads down for an early night we were rudely awakened from our sweet dreams by the sound of a verbal bombshell going off in our ears. Eddie addressed us, 'In a short while you will be going on the 'Long Drag' and your bergens will be upped to 55 pounds. From reading up beforehand, I had an idea what was in store for us, a march of around forty miles in twenty hours or under. People may read this and say 'No problem,' but believe me, after having slept very little the previous night, then climbing Ben Lomond twice, and now after a few hours rest, diving straight into this marathon journey, believe me when I say that 'the alarm bells were ringing LOUDLY!' It was going to take some serious willpower to pull this one off.

We set off at ten-minute intervals, the slowest leaving first, right back to Karl who would be leaving last. I think I was fourth or fifth from the back, and could not wait to get started. We were allowed to use roads and tracks which the guys on a proper Selection would probably be binned for. I think the SAS were putting safety first, as the thought of navigating over the hills at night seemed daunting (if not impossible) to most. 10.15 pm, and off into the dark I marched. We were told not to use the obvious track out of camp, (advice which many volunteers chose to ignore) so a sharp right and right again took you over a field, through a forest, then onto the main road towards the little town of Aberfoyle. Quietly, I cursed as I crashed through sharp branches, marshy pools and thick undergrowth following a general compass bearing. You are always very wary of making a navigational mistake especially at the starting point. A big fuck-up here could be costly in time and wasted energy. The two extra bricks in the pack became more noticeable, especially after leaving the camp where there were two large fences to negotiate upon which I nearly twisted my leg out of the socket. The weight just pulled you over if you lost your balance. I constantly checked my map just to be ultra-certain of reaching the road. Once onto the road, it was a case of getting into a rhythm of jog march, jog march. I tried to put in a reasonably quick start and get some miles in as tiredness would definitely be a telling factor later. A few miles from camp I passed a big mansion-type house, which was perched on a setting high above the level of the road. The garden ran for some length and was lined with short trees, which were evenly spaced behind an old-fashioned iron fence. The reason for explaining the relevance of this particular house I will now divulge. My mind was busy concentrating on locating the proper turn-off for the road which would eventually lead me to the first RV when I suddenly became aware of some low growling noises. These quickly turned to very aggressive barking at which point I realised I had two large Rottwiellers taking an instant disliking to my presence. 'Oh, shit!' I trembled, 'these two fuckers think I'm a family size tin of Pedigree Chum.' I thought 'this has to be a set up.' The only options readily available were to swim past them in the loch on my right, which was not a good idea with the fridge on the back, but I suppose drowning would have been a less painful way to die! The other was to take them on in a good old fistfight. I reasoned, 'maybe trying to kid them by making the gun noises you did when you played soldiers as a child would work.' Somehow, I don't think these monsters were going to fall for that one. I think the SLR rifle was the main reason for them going nuts in the first place. The frightening thing was that they could have at any time if they had wished to do so, just slip through the large spacing in the fence. I just kept walking not daring to take my eyes off of them as they followed me the length of the garden. In the end it was all nothing but loud noise made by a couple of rather large dogs full of empty threats. Unfortunately though I would just have to put up with the squidgy mess in my pants for the rest of the march! Speaking to some of the guys afterwards, none of them had seen or heard of the dogs. 'Was I going crazy?'

As I left the town of Aberfoyle behind I stared upwards in awe at the thousands of stars sparkling in the black sky and thought of how insignificant we all were in the vastness of the universe. Just a bunch of ants carrying packs of bricks on a little winding road somewhere in central Scotland. I felt a real inner happiness and smiled to myself as I let my thoughts wander around on a spiritual journey. Weather-wise we really could not have asked for a better night.

I now began to catch up with and pass little groups of people who had left before me and I felt greatly encouraged although there was still a long, long way to go. I offered a quick 'Hi' or 'Alright' on the way but responses were fairly subdued. The miles slowly rolled by as did a million crazy thoughts and finally, the first objective was within sight. Two contestants, Cass and Rimma were just ahead of me as I arrived at RV 1, which was a quiet lay-by at the side of the road. Eight miles in around two hours and I was feeling good. To my quiet astonishment we were among the first in, which from a personal point of view was very heartening given that most of the others had left before me. Dr Stroud was there to make sure that people were okay to carry on and to tend to any minor injuries. I took the opportunity to fill my water bottle then marched over to a Land Rover where the DS gave me the next grid reference. A few bodies were beginning to appear just as I stole off into the loneliness of the night but importantly, none of the front runners were among them. I had taken off sharp and wasted no time in checking sore feet or an aching back. What was the point? Pain was going to be our companion for the duration so I put my mind to letting 'him' tag along with me. At this point I wasn't sure if any of the others were ahead of me so I set myself the challenge of putting on a steady pace and seeing if I could catch anyone. The next RV was eleven miles away and would be a very tough leg as it was taking us through the wee small hours when the mind and body would be waning in willpower and energy. I could take comfort from the fact that the journey ahead was on road then track and not over hill and moor in the black of night. All I had to do was keep an eye on the map and get the turn off at a little place called Brig O' Turk - simple. Well ... I missed the bloody turn off!

CHAPTER 5

Day 3

Northern Lights and Mental Fights

The loch was glistening through the trees and a perfect calm atmosphere made for a truly relaxing feeling inside. The smell of forestry and good fresh air streamed through my nose and filled my lungs. At some point, I reckoned Karl, Jonathon and Lee would be pounding up behind me, putting the pressure on and upping the pace. Still there was no sign of anyone. I checked my watch in relation to the distance I had covered and it was at that moment that some doubt began creeping into my mind. I seemed to have been walking for too long and felt that I should have located the turn-off long before now. My torch shone on a small sign half-covered by thick bushes where I read the Gaelic name of some farm or house. A quick look at the map revealed the nightmare scenario of a disastrous navigating error. I'd been daydreaming a bit and was, in all honesty, looking for the Brig o' Turk signpost in flashing neon lights, saying 'This way!' I was absolutely mad with myself, cursing to anything and nothing all at the same time. By the time I did get back on track I'd lost about twenty-five minutes of valuable time.

After a swift interview with the BBC crew I was back on the proper bearing and it wasn't too long before I began passing some bodies for the second time that night. My feet were in quite a bit of pain now no thanks to the many miles on a hard, unforgiving tarmac surface and the large pack bore down heavily on my size 9's. I had made a critical error on choice of boots to wear opting for my old Karrimor KSB's due to the fact that they were slightly lighter. The new KSB's I had purchased a few months ago were well broken in before the programme and would have saved me a lot of discomfort. Luckily I had thrown them in with my kit just in case, and a few days later I managed to sneak into the holding area and swap them over. It was like putting on slippers. For now though it was a case of 'switch off' and keep bloody moving as fast as possible!

Earlier on I mentioned the subject of walking on your own and the weird experiences and situations it throws up, and on this occasion it must have been the lack of sleep and forced exertion, which placed the mind in a crazy, hallucinatory state. Added to this physically, the pack was now biting hard into the shoulders and simply carrying the rifle became a constant pain in the arse, probably because I don't often carry one on a normal jaunt in the hills! I remember midway through the punishing third leg of 'Long Drag' passing a tree (one like the ones they always have in the horror movies) and for a second or two thinking it looked like a huge man striding towards me, about to smother me. Spooky! Little 'incidents' like these helped you laugh at yourself and distract you from the pain and tiredness.

One experience more memorable during that long night, than any of those, which involved suffering or hallucinating, was the awesome phenomenon known to man as the aurora borealis or Northern Lights. Away in the night sky, a green glow mingled and danced with the stars and broad beams of light descended earthwards on a massive scale, which at first I thought were vapour trails from alien spaceships finally coming to take over our world. Someone had either spiked the water in the streams or I was going completely off my rocker! 'It was probably the latter.' Once the brain started functioning properly again, the thought of sheer beauty at being a tiny molecule in a vast Universe was mind-blowing and totally overwhelming. To view an astonishing spectacle like this for the first time, given the circumstances we were in was in many ways, spiritually uplifting. Another experience I'll never forget in my life.

By now my pace was slowing a little and a few of the lads caught up, so we were virtually walking in a small group. It went against my own strict principles for accomplishing the march alone but there just simply wasn't any acceleration in the tank at that particular time. We stopped for five minutes to get a biscuit and a piece of chocolate down our necks and each man had to fight his own demons against the over-powering urge to fall asleep. We then left the track as the bearing altered and headed uphill, looking for a path marked clearly on the map. Obscenities filled the air as we constantly stumbled and tripped over large heather tussocks, the odd sharp rock, and numerous potholes in a kind of non-explosive minefield. On and on it seemed to go with the darkness playing mind tricks in relation to distance judgement.

The headlights of a vehicle spotted away to our left on a hill track could only mean one thing - the DS. On seeing our torchlight's they drove on and within a short time, drew up to within shouting distance where they asked if everything was all right and would we like a brew. 'No thanks Staff, everything's fine.' It would have been a sign of weakness to accept, and happily everyone declined what was at the time, a bloody good offer!

It was not long now until first light on what had proven to be an extremely hard and testing journey through the night but spirits were definitely anticipating the lift with which it would bring. And that is exactly what happened. Words were exchanged only briefly during the section we walked together, but there was certainly a spring in everyone's step as full daylight came in. We arrived at the second checkpoint to see Karl and Jonathon resting by a bridge, along with Matt who'd arrived just before us. We checked in with the DS then the few contestants who had made it this far, prepared for the next strength-sapping leg of the torturous challenge. Karl and Jonathon gave off the impression that they were fed and rested after having stuck together through the tricky route-finding part of the march. They had already been given the next grid reference whereupon both of them took off in completely opposite directions. The tall gangly frame of Jonathon sped off on a track to our left. He looked very capable and strong and had produced a very good display so far. My first impressions of him (apart from briefly chatting at the fitness test) were that of a confident, slightly arrogant, outspoken and very determined individual. He chose a route which initially defied logical thinking, but in fact, very nearly paid a rewarding dividend had it not been for a tightly packed forest plantation which became a nightmare maze of flesh-tearing dead-ends.

I gathered my thoughts and muttered to myself, 'Not too bad after the balls-up back at the Brig O' Turk.' As part of the bigger picture, I felt things were going reasonably well at that point in time. Strangely, the little group I had come in with and another group, who literally appeared out of nowhere, was ordered to 'get some scoff down our necks and rest up.' Dr Stroud was on hand with some blister pads and quietly questioned contestants' general well being. Personally, there was no problem with blisters on my feet, but the pressure on the soles of them was giving me some anxiety. I would honestly have preferred to crack on but we were told the time we spent in holding would be taken off from our final finishing time - I don't know if it ever was, but I reckon I was there around forty-five minutes to an hour. A cooked meal tasted lovely as it passed over the taste buds, even though it was crap food. Curry, Bovril, rice and two packets of soup all mixed in, followed by porridge and chocolate powder, would usually be a fairly low choice of cuisine on the menu at home but today the calories were being thrown in, big style. Before we started enjoying the rest too much though, the DS shouted for us to be ready to leave.

It had felt good getting the Bergens off of our backs and having our feet out to air, but now shoulders, back and feet complained bitterly as the gear went back on. The rest was in many ways counterproductive, as the human mind seems to find every excuse possible to avoid action after rest, following a sustained period of severe physical activity.

The next checkpoint didn't seem too bad at all after studying the map. I didn't really want to say to the others when they asked, which direction I was taking, but in the end they all chose different routes anyway and I was back where I wanted to be, on my own! Not because I'm a loner, just the fact that that's what the exercise was all about. Although I took the straight A to B direct route which meant traversing over a high pass, the gamble was that the lower ground might have been boggy and hard going. It wasn't, and worked out a treat. The wee songs returned in my head as I got down to concentrating on getting the miles in and beating the twenty-hour mark. A section about a mile or two of peat bogs and deep heather on the high ground was the only area of rough going, that is apart from the constant mental 'war' against the pain. By now my feet were absolutely throbbing but I just had to grit the teeth and go harder. As I approached the checkpoint I made a point of looking my best, nice and tidy, showing no signs of decline (outwardly or inwardly) and marching in good order. Well that was the idea anyway. I probably looked like a bag of shit! At this stage (I think it was the 26 mile point) fitness was out the window, it was a mental game now. 'Keep going, c'mon keep going,' over and over it went like a programmed voice in my head. I was feeling rather chuffed with myself and was quite sure I would be first in after seeing where the others had gone. Most had opted for an 'easier looking' route which followed a low-level track, but took a huge dog-leg detour in order to reach the RV. I could not believe it when I saw Karl relaxing by a tree. I was absolutely stunned. 'What a machine.' To be fair, he did have quite a sizeable start on those of us who had been held at RV 2 but I soon found out he'd already been on his way up the next hill and inexplicably, had to be brought back by helicopter. In a sheltered, wooded area by the side of the road we had a brew and chatted, then slipped into our sleeping bags to await further orders. Things did not look good at all with Karl being pulled back, and although I myself had been given the next grid reference also, we were going nowhere and it was some time before the first of the exhausted, weary bodies started to trickle in.

I reckoned that with the stoppage time (RV 2) taken off and the fourteen miles still to travel, I had maybe four-and-a-half to five hours to complete 'Long Drag'. Who knows? I still find myself (over two years after that gruelling march) transporting my mind back to that very day and wondering if I could have done it within the designated time. I certainly would not have given up, but for now sadly, the march was abandoned much to the annoyance of the DS, Karl and of course myself. It may sound masochistic but I definitely wanted to do the 'big one'. Endurance or Long Drag is undoubtedly one of THE toughest military challenges in the world and it would have been nice just for personal satisfaction to know that you had endured it.

The main reason for the march being prematurely terminated was that people were strung out all over the place and there simply wasn't the resources and 'people on the ground' to cover such a wide area. After what seemed like hours, quite a few bodies had now gathered in the trees and were swapping stories when the ominous figure of Eddie Stone appeared up on the road with the look of a raging bull. Behind him trailed three very sullen-looking characters who'd just had a major bollocking for having a little sing-song. Apparently, they'd decided to put on a show for the BBC as they came into the checkpoint and impressively belted out an American-style drill song while holding their 'nuts'. The DS were not impressed and went nuts themselves while Eddie made them sing it all over again to our assembled company. It was like a scene from that old TV programme 'It Ain't Half Hot Mum' except this was not funny at all, (well not for the trio of performers anyway). Quietly, the rest of us had a chuckle although we made sure Eddie couldn't see us. We thought and they thought it was curtains for them but luckily when the dismissals came later, they were spared the agony of being booted out. I think Eddie may have had a little laugh to himself afterwards – then again, maybe not!

The DS had lost patience playing the waiting game as many more volunteers were still unaccounted for. The first four or five of us were told to get our arses into a Land Rover. It was time to go again, but to where we knew not. Eddie was at the wheel of our vehicle and took off like a man possessed, kicking up gravel and stones as he threw the Land Rover expertly along the very narrow and winding road. On one such blind bend each of us thought that our time had come and watched as St Peter opened the gates to welcome us into heaven. As Eddie thrashed into a corner full on, hearts went into mouths as a car appeared straight in front of us. Our driver never batted an eyelid as he hammered the brake then deftly turned the wheel sharply left, bypassing the other car on the tightest of angles. There was certainly no room for error as the verge sloped downwards towards Loch Katrine. We all looked at each other in the back with shit-filled trousers, but no one dared say a word.

The late afternoon sun shone on the loch as we sped around its shores and into the unknown. We were asked what we thought was next, but no one quite knew what to expect. Canoeing, swimming, more marching? Eventually, we were led down to a small bay on the loch side and given the good news. A mock river crossing over a stretch of water, some 25 metres in distance where we were to strip down to our underpants and use the Bergens as floatation aids. An amusing situation arose when two of the girls commented that they were improperly (or properly to the lads) dressed for stripping off, with one having only a thong on and the other with absolutely nothing! The DS kindly let them keep their combat trousers on, much to the dismay of the rest of us.

Thankfully, the bricks were taken out for this test, or we would have been doing some scuba-diving without the oxygen on the bed of the loch. Everything was put into a bin liner and tightly sealed then the rifle was placed on the top of the makeshift float. Now we were prepared and ready to swim over. One by one we crossed to the other side taking great care not to drop the weapon into the depths below, for we were politely informed of the consequences, 'You'll be swimming down for it yourselves!'

The water was very cold even though it was late summer, but it had a lovely soothing effect on aching limbs and feet. Once I had successfully completed the task I carefully made my way over the sharp rocks and quickly dried myself off. It was at that moment I looked around and realised how few of us were left from the group which had started the night before. Faces (my own included) displayed signs of tiredness and fatigue, but everyone seemed to be past caring. For a final sting in the tail, the DS gave us a little beasting. 'That pylon up there on the hillside. Get up to it as fast as possible,' he said. We took off over the swampy, sandy mud then hit the steep incline of the hill, clawing and scraping to get up. That bloody pylon seemed like it was on top of Everest as lactic acid filled the muscles of the thighs and calves. As we reassembled the sounds of heavy breathing and panting spewed out from people as everyone tried desperately to generate some saliva into their bone-dry mouths. 'Right, get back up there! I said run didn't I, what are you waiting for?' I thought my lungs were being sprayed with a flame-thrower as we scrambled up once more, then slid and fell back down again.

'OK, off you go again!' Everyone obeyed, but this time they called us back after a few yards. I felt they were just testing our resolve and willpower and making sure we were up for it. After what we'd gone through over the past thirty-six hours or so we could finally relax. Physically, but not mentally. I don't know about the others but I always had the 'alert' button switched on, ready for anything. Back at camp it was time for fresh rations and a good chat although at the back of everyone's minds, the spectre of dismissals hung menacingly in the air. A special mention must go to the girls, not to patronise them but to honestly acknowledge some good old blood and guts effort. They had the offer before setting off on the Long Drag to opt for a 35-pound pack instead of the 55 pounds but chose by a democratic vote to go 'heavy', thus proving that they could match the guys when it came to load carrying.

While we sat outside the tents gorging our food, stories began circulating around where we heard of people settling down in the heather and having a few hours kip through the night, and of others who hitched a lift from a local farmer to illegally ease the long, painful miles. I suppose everyone had their own gameplans to get them through what was undoubtedly a fearsome challenge, a real test on the human body. The name on most peoples' lips was of course Karl's. He had produced two outstanding performances in the hills and already some contestants had him picked as the winner. He was certainly looking strong and seemed to possess the proper attitude but there were many obstacles still to cross and many assaults on the character still to come.

Parade was called later in the evening and the intimidating voice and figure of Staff Sergeant Eddie Stone struck fear into us all once more. The roll call of names being dismissed was cleverly staged with sufficient pause for effect. On and on it went with eight going in total. We were later told that the SAS would have decimated the numbers due to people under-performing but the BBC had had a 'word in their ear' arguing that there would be no show left if it carried on like this. Surprisingly, some contestants remained in the line-up that hadn't taken part in the river crossing and beasting. One of those dismissed, Rosie was from our tent but myself and the lads would always be indebted to her for her kindness and generosity. On arriving back in camp after Long Drag she had set about cooking up some food for us and unselfishly gave up her rations. It was very much appreciated at a time when we were all slightly shattered.

    I think I was probably sleeping before I unzipped my bag and wormed my way into 'quilted heaven' - already dreaming of the 'delights' which lay ahead tomorrow.

CHAPTER 6

Day 4

Take you on a Walk Through HELL!

The weather had been uncharacteristically warm and sunny for an unbroken spell going back days. Today would be different. Good old Scottish rain and mist was back with a vengeance, but perfect for the task, which lay ahead. We were taken to a location not far from the camp, in a forested area and given a basic lesson in survival techniques. We listened intently to what Barry Davies had to tell us and observed the different kinds of shelters which could be put together utilising the natural surroundings on offer. It was great listening to a true expert in his field and during a lighter moment, he told us of some of his funnier stories and situations. He'd also hinted at the possibility of a parachute jump, should any of us progress to the next stage. This news had everyone quietly buzzing with excitement.

Some of us thought that today (because of the slightly relaxed manner and forestry surroundings in which we found ourselves) we'd be building a lovely little replica SAS shelter and possibly living a night inside it being at one with nature and all that. How wrong could we have been? Back at camp we were issued with an old army Greatcoat and had our smocks taken from us, leaving us with just a thin, base-layer top on. I was so glad I had brought my lightweight, quick-drying thermal tops. These garments are the business, keeping you comfortably warm with the capacity to dry very quickly after considerable exertion. We were also allowed a woolly hat and that was basically it.

I'm sure we didn't have breakfast that morning, all part of the bigger picture, which we were soon to find out about.

'This morning you are going on a little Escape and Evasion exercise, taking on the role of POW's. You will be split into four teams of four and each team will be given a sketch map, a button compass, a survival tin and a RV point to check in at no later than 5pm.' The DS gave us a couple of minutes to sort ourselves out. Everyone made a beeline for their tents and stuffed as much food into their mouths as was humanly possible. If you were caught with anything other than what had been issued, you were in trouble. I'm sure I broke the world record for stuffing a full packet of dextrose sweets and two Mars Bars into my mouth. As Eddie called us back on parade we must have been a sight, cheeks full to the gunnels, chomping away furiously on the last food we'd taste for a long time. I'm sure he knew what everyone was up to, it was simply an initiative there to be seized. The Land Rovers raced off with us in the back, taking us on a trip, which I don't think any souls that were there, will ever forget. Our team consisted of Colin, Cassius, Paul and myself, with Colin being designated team leader. It was a fairly strong squad considering the nick of some of the others' feet. Some contestants could not believe we were going hiking again for a long distance over rough country. Eddie pointed to a spot on our map with a blade of grass and made sure we were all aware of our destination. I have no doubt in my mind, whatsoever, that we went to the correct RV we were given. More about this fact shortly.

The first team took off, in what direction we knew not. Starting times were staggered, so unless you chose a similar route, you were not going to see the others. Attempting to capture us soon would be the DS, a Search and Rescue team with dogs and a regiment of Argyle and Sutherland Highlanders although we thought Eddie threw that one in for a laugh, but all the same we had to take it seriously enough. The call came to 'GO' and we charged out of the vehicle like a mob of psychopath's let loose for a day. Over a field and up to the tree line we ran, while overhead a helicopter filmed our moves. It was only then when the initial adrenaline died away, we remembered how sore our feet were from the previous hammering they'd taken. Some of us had first-aid kits but were not allowed access to our gear, therefore it was impossible to tape up our feet properly for the big days in the hills, and more importantly, the long miles covered on tarmac roads and hard metal tracks. During Long Drag the doctors did what they could, patching people's feet up with blister pads, but the damage was already done.

We made our way to a break in the forest, which was a good choice meaning once found we could plan a more direct route to the RV. The BBC had given all of the teams a small video camera for the purpose of filming ourselves as the action unfolded. The little burden was more of a nuisance than anything but each of us agreed to carry it in turns and do a spot of 'out in the field reporting'. Big Colin in particular excelled in his Kate Adie-type role and did a superb job interviewing us. He should have been working for the BBC. At one point we had considered taking a route by the road which may have saved some miles over deep heather but thought better of it, having been instructed to stay clear of all traffic, houses and population in general. After a few miles Cass pulled a Mars Bar from his underpants and divided it into four pieces. I'm sure it WAS chocolate and not something else he'd done earlier! He'd hidden it when he was in the tent and now, shared it unselfishly between us. We gave a wide berth to a farm house and later some hillwalkers who were out and about on our chosen route. I thought it strange, the activity, for what I reckoned was a quiet area but nonetheless we played the game. We also spotted what looked like the DS tracking our moves from a hillside. I kept the map and compass throughout, constantly checking and re-checking our route but always we made decisions as a group. Cass, who'd never done map reading before, hinted that he was keen to learn and received a quick lesson en route. Colin led a good team and we were all getting along really well, when he went and blew it. Well into the march we decided to blacken ourselves with some peat from a bog and darken any white or shiny bits of clothing. Colin decided to stick big clumps of grass and heather into his jacket lapels and hat, which made him look like a human bush. He resembled one of the guys from the old TV sitcom - Dad's Army. We all fell about, pissing ourselves laughing at his costume but the panel of judge's awarded 10 out of 10 for effort.

By now we were well on schedule to reach the RV at five o'clock and began to tread more warily. Fine drizzle had started to fall, followed by low cloud, and finally, a stiff breeze. Now we were in it. Paul spotted the gate at the top corner of the forest, which we'd navigated to precision. There was no one around so we approached quietly, checking everywhere for the first signs of a trap, and made ready to leg it. We circumnavigated the forest line for a few hundred metres just to make sure we had not missed the checkpoint then we had a heated debate concerning our next move. In the end, we hopped the gate and lay low under some pine trees for ten to fifteen minutes waiting to see if the DS were going to appear but no one did. After another debate we decided to head for a gate maybe half a mile away where there was plenty of activity, but decided against that when we saw dogs and guys with orange outfits on. The hunter force were obviously there. We were told later that we should still have made for the RV but unaware of the rules of the exercise, we made the decision to go on the run, fuck the RV! Mist gathered thick all around us now so we hurried down the track then took the direction heading away from the bodies we'd spotted. While crossing a bridge over a gorge someone had the bright idea of making it our home for the night. It was perfect. There was just enough room for the four of us to perch on a ledge underneath the solid structure of old railway sleepers. Less than five feet in front of us the ledge dropped steeply away into the raging torrent below. Colin spotted a good supply of dead wood on the other side of the gorge which we collected in for the purpose of getting a fire going in the morning. Some home improvements were necessary as rainwater constantly dripped in through the cracks above and found its way down onto our exposed necks. A few large clumps of grass soon plugged the offending gaps.

Paul, who was the youngest among us seemed quite flappy by now and wanted to go against the group decision to stay put. 'I say we should go up to the other gate lads,' he pleaded. 'Nah, fuck that man' said Cass. 'We'll only succeed in turning ourselves in!'

As far as Colin and I were concerned, Cass was right. We'd been given survival training and as we were out for the night, this was as good a place as any to stay. We snuggled together for warmth like four little puppies in a basket and set our minds on getting through what would be a long, hungry and altogether miserable night. As we had ceased being active some time ago, our damp clothing began to feel very uncomfortable and our bodies' core temperatures were in danger of dropping into the 'hypothermic' zone. Cass constantly asked to have the fire lit, but that was simply not on. We would only have succeeded in compromising our position, although it did seem a bloody good idea! Five minutes before 8.00pm, we heard some footsteps pass right over our heads. Instantly the four of us were alert. 'It's OK they've passed,' whispered Colin. As we settled back down, Cass spotted a black and white Collie dog on the other side of the gorge in the area where we'd been collecting the wood. We found out later that the search team were on the heels of Karl's team (who'd passed over our heads) and were diverted by that intelligent little dog now sniffing about in a frenzy. 'Fuck off dog,' whispered Cass, but it was no use - they were on to us. Adrenaline started to pump through our bodies as we waited for the inevitable. A dog handler then appeared in our view, following his dog's lead, and started searching around. We sat there motionless, hoping he would not look over. There was a combined sense of panic and excitement to add to the drama of the situation. With one quick glance over by the handler, our game was up. He shouted 'BBC, you're caught!' We must have looked like scared rabbits caught in a car's headlights. Cass then came up with a classic statement, 'When they come down for us, let's get stuck into them.' And to emphasize his point he said 'There are four of us.' He was told without hesitation to 'Fuck right off, you're on your own mate!' Another bright idea came to him when quick as a flash, he got the video camera out and started filming as the SAS jumped down and manhandled us back up to the track. In the circumstances it was hilarious but there was no fucking about, no friendly 'That's you caught lads,' from these guys. I was pulled up from above like a rag doll being grabbed by an over-zealous child and laid flat out on the bridge which we had been hiding under. Breathing was heavy and hearts pumped furiously as we lay side by side, the cold puddles of water, seeping through our clothes and onto our skin. 'Keep your fucking heads down!' screamed the DS.

A minute passed by and I took a quick glance around to see the DS about twenty metres away. I sprang up, shouted to the others to do likewise, and legged it down the track and off into the mist. I reckon Linford Christie would have struggled to keep up. A couple of hundred metres on, I swerved off the track and into some deep heather, trying desperately to control my breathing. I even threw clumps of heather over me to camouflage myself. Then I thought, 'What the hell are you doing, you silly bastard.' I think I'd been reading too many books which stated, 'When captured, try to plan your escape sooner rather that later.' We were told when caught, that that was it, no 'taking off' or 'resisting capture'. I'd just risked breaking the rules and possibly being binned but luckily for me, Cass was told to 'Go and get your daft mate.' There now entered a very strange period, which my mind could not make clear sense of. I followed Cass back to the bridge and spotted Colin and Paul in a press-up position with the DS standing close by. Cass mimicked the DS's accent perfectly and told the guys to give him ten (press-ups) which they duly did. I thought 'You bastard, you've changed sides.' He paused, then said 'OK, now roll onto your backs and bark like dogs.' If they had done that one I swear I would have collapsed and died with laughter. Even the DS laughed, then he pulled himself together and told Cass and myself to join in with the press-ups. I still had it in my mind, Cass had changed sides, I don't know why.

    We were then led up the track to the gate, which we had seen earlier, and could hear Eddie's voice along with some others. By now hoods had been placed over our heads and the Greatcoats and woolly hats had been taken from us. Darkness had also set in. I was able to make out vehicle headlights and bodies moving about through the thin material of the hood. I wasn't sure if I was the only one who could see through the hood, but kept my mouth shut in any case. As I lay on the ground I remember my breathing starting to go out of control, a combination of the cold penetrating my chest and the stress caused by the difficulty of breathing through a hood. I was on the verge of panic.

    'C'mon pull yourself together or you'll be out,' I told myself. 'Big deep breaths.' The DS kept hitting us with questions, trying to make us crack, as we were only allowed to give six proper answers. Any questions outside of those six was answered with 'I can't answer that question sir.' Various ploys were tried as were disorientating methods, then came the stress positions. A casual lean on the cold metalwork of a vehicle may seem a doddle until you're there for fifteen to twenty minutes at a time with the DS constantly checking your position to see there's no cheating. My hands were starting to go numb. The muscles in my upper arms were on fire, but I found the experience a great mental challenge. To take my mind away I used a simple ploy, much like counting sheep at bed time. Count to one hundred steadily, then repeat the whole process over and over, and then vary the multiples counted. All sense of time was beginning to go as we were bundled into a Land Rover and taken on a very long, disorientating drive. Not a word was spoken, each man left with his own thoughts. Every now and then I'd think of Cass imitating the DS and start sniggering like the dog 'Mutley' from the 'Wacky Races' cartoon. It was a real struggle to stop myself from producing an all out belly laugh though I don't think that would have gone down too well with our captors. Speaking to some of the others after the ordeal, we thought at this point, 'Wow, that was hard, now we'll get to our cosy, warm beds.' In the immortal words of Billy Conolly 'Oh, do you bloody think so?' Really, the 'game' had just begun. The trapdoor to Hell swung open and pulled us in!

CHAPTER 7

Day 5

Mind Games.

The Land Rover finally came to a halt and I sat there thinking, 'Where the hell are we?' Colin said to me later that he knew we were back at the farm where our camp was, but for me, the disorientating drive had done the trick. I did not have a clue. One by one, the four of us were taken from the vehicle at different intervals, then put into a stress position on the ground. You were left kneeling on the stony surface with your hands placed across your head and elbows raised. I was aware of the other three nearby, all of us going through our own hell. The rain and cold penetrated once more, as all feeling in the lower limbs just vanished. I kept talking to myself, keeping my mind alert, while the psychological games went on around us. Footsteps would come rushing up to you, then just stop and stand for a bit, or wander round and back and forth. I could hear the running water of a stream and reckoned we would definitely be heading in there at some point. It was all very confusing, which was the whole idea I suppose. I must have been down on my knees for what seemed like forty-five minutes to an hour when the interrogators finally came and lifted me. My legs refused to operate, so I ended up being dragged. I could make out a bright light shining through the hood. It was a small tent and once inside, the hood was lifted from my face to be confronted by an image you would imagine on a horror film, (or that's how my mind saw it). I stood face to face with a Dr Frankenstein-type character. He said in a clear even tone, 'I am a doctor, I cannot be impersonated. The next time you see me, it will all be over. Do you understand?'

'I cannot answer that question sir,' I replied. I was eventually persuaded he was a genuine doctor, then it was down with the hood and back outside. The whole situation seemed very surreal. You really had the feeling you were there but you were not. It was real crazy stuff! I kept telling myself 'Keep your mind your own, nothing's gonna penetrate.' I was led across what seemed like a courtyard and taken into the 'Mind Games Mecca' for some real fun. Through the hood I could make out what seemed to be the inside of some kind of hangar or warehouse. It must have been after midnight, but like I say, time was hard to keep track of. The first thing to hit you was the bump, bump, bump, like a kind of techno beat music but not really any kind of specific music. It was pounding white noise and it did your head in after a while. I could also make out others in the building and realised some teams must have been compromised and I wondered how long they had been here.

It was straight into stress positions, simple everyday actions (not that I'm implying people practice these positions) like leaning on a wall with one arm or sitting with a straight back, and hands placed on top of your head. Each of these lasted around twenty minutes and there were plenty of variations for us to try! The kind of thing which doesn't sound at all like hard work, but the longer you held them, the more your muscles burned, and any sagging was leapt upon and instantly corrected by rough hands or a boot to widen your stance. I must admit, I was thoroughly enjoying this mental challenge. Hunger reared its head on many occasions but had to be swept away. I think dwelling on the likes of a Big Mac and large French Fries would have just thrown you over the edge. Just when you were starting to doze a little, something would crash off the wall or a large metal object would clang off the concrete floor and bring you right back to reality. Then it was time for some questioning. You were dragged away like a sheep being pulled from the safety of the flock, by a hungry wolf. Away from the constant beat of the music (if you could call it that) normality returned for a split second until you were planted down on a seat to face a professional interrogator. I remember being blinded by the lights in the room which all added to the very real atmosphere of being captured. The interrogator started 'What's your name?' 'Gary,' I replied. 'You must have a surname, what is it?' 'I can't answer that question sir.' And so started the game of 'Cat and Mouse' where only the six answers were allowed, which were- name, next of kin, age, occupation, where you lived, and blood group. It wasn't much to remember, but the wording of questions was sometimes turned slightly to make you trip up and with physical and mental fatigue kicking in, you had to be really switched on. I gave him nothing, or not that I was aware of, so it was back to 'stressville'. I kept saying to myself 'Yeah, give me more. There's no way I'm gonna break.' The whole ordeal was really just a battle with your own mind. We were never physically abused but whatever they were going to throw at you it was a case of keeping your mind in good shape. The minute you started thinking it was too tough or too much to handle, that was it for you. A negative avalanche would engulf you and swallow you up. On and on and on it dragged. Boredom was another strong foe to keep at bay. I used the tried and tested little tricks to keep on top like, singing songs in my head, spelling any word which came to me and of course counting to a hundred repeatedly. The next time I was taken in the interrogator changed his tactics and exploded in my face with a show of aggression. I sat there calm and confident, then said inwardly, 'Fuck you mate, you ain't getting nothing.' A glass of water or juice was offered but I refused to take it. We were told later, to take something when offered, but at the time I didn't want to risk it. 'OK, get him out of here!' he barked.

Off I went, back to the hellhole with no let up whatsoever in the psychological warfare. You'd be holding a stress position then bang! One of our captors would grab you and move you ten feet or so, then you'd be put into a squat with your arms in front of you, and a heavy bar placed in them. At times, the shaking was uncontrollable, as overworked muscles struggled to function any more. The hours wore on, and the urge to just topple over and sleep on the concrete floor became very strong. I've never taken drugs before, but some of the hallucinations I was having in the latter stages were unbelievable. One in particular was when I was leaning on the wall and a shadow from the person next to me, 'came alive' and started moving like a limbo dancer. The barn wall had also become decorated with lovely flowery wallpaper. Even in the exhausted state I was in, I found myself giggling away at the absurd situation, which I was embroiled in. 'This is not real. Maybe it is real.' The mind was playing mental tennis, back and forth, trying to make sense of it all. As time passed by the thought of needing the toilet came to the fore. 'What will I do?' I hadn't had the toilet for hours, but the fact that we had not eaten all day or drunk fluid for a very long time helped in some ways. The more I thought, the more I started to need a pee. 'Well sod it, if I need to pee or shit, the trousers will do nicely.' Again we weren't sure of the rules but were informed later that it was OK to put the hand up as a signal.

In I went for questioning for a third time. Same routine again although this time, a piece of paper was placed in front of me and I was asked to sign it, which I promptly did. Later I was informed of the gravity of this blunder as I could have been signing for anything be it explosives, murder or a whole host of manufactured crimes.

After a quicker than normal session I was taken back out and led into the 'white noise' disco but after a short time I was grabbed for the final walk to freedom. The hood was lifted and 'Dr. Frankenstein' confronted me once more. The glare from the camera lights was overpowering as I listened to the psychiatrist tell me it was all over. 'I can't answer that question sir.' I replied. He had to convince me a few times that it REALLY was all over.

One of the SAS guys said 'Well done' which was a nice touch considering that these lads go through a much longer and tougher process than we had. Still, I felt very pleased that I'd challenged myself and won and thought my performance had been good enough to pass. We wouldn't know till later that day who amongst us had cracked under the severe mental pressure but first, it was time to chill out and try to get the brains back into a semi-normal state. I entered a building, climbed a set of stairs then suddenly registered where we had been detained. It was Drumlean Farm, the place of our base camp. I could not believe it. The farm office felt lovely and warm as I walked into the friendly atmosphere of some familiar faces, BBC crew members amongst them. We all acknowledged and congratulated each other on reaching the end of the tunnel and finding the light. Many faces were absent from the company, either still on the run or still being interrogated, poor buggers! The BBC told us the experience was not a nice one to witness at all but they seemed genuinely surprised at how cheery we were considering the immense pressure we had all been under. At one stage they even talked about pulling the plug and getting us the hell out of there. They would have had to take me biting and scratching. There was no way I, or indeed any of the others would have wanted the exercise to end in such a way.

I would not have missed that for the world, an absolutely fantastic experience. We were given plates of hot soup and buttered rolls and promptly washed those down with cups of tea and Mars Bars. It tasted as good as any food a world class chef could prepare, believe me! I wandered down the short distance to camp feeling completely at one with the Universe. It sounds corny but until you're tested in certain circumstances in life, you never know what great feelings the mind is capable of experiencing. The spotlights of the camp could mean only one thing as they came into view - tent, sleeping bag ... sleep.

My watch told me it was 04.30am and I lay for a second thinking. 'What the hell's next? Surely, they would give us time to rest. Who knows?' I told myself 'Don't get complacent, be ready for anything.' We heard later that day, that Karl's team had not been caught until around midnight, so they were not released until around 07.00am. which was a great effort. The real plaudits and praise must go to the SAS guys for the totally unrelenting pressure they kept up and also the sheer professionalism in which they carried out their task. There was never a moment's rest throughout, never a time when you could have a mental breather. These lads would need some serious rest also.

I awoke thinking I had had a great night's sleep only to glance at my watch and see it was 07.30am. I had a grand total of three hours but for some strange reason felt no more tired or fatigued than on any other day. Another half-hour and I was up, having a brew and scoffing some porridge and chocolate mix. The camp seemed still and very peaceful, only the birds melodic chirping from perches in the trees scattered around broke the silence. I couldn't believe I was up and not still zonked out in my sleeping bag. Nic, Lee and Dave were still sound, sleeping like babies. I wondered if they were having pleasant dreams or mixing it in the darker side, maybe playing characters in a real-life video game with no way out. I sorted over the details of my own experience from start to finish and questioned my performance. I was content in the fact that I, and we as a team had performed everything as best we could and hoped it would be enough to get through to the next stage.

People began to surface and gradually we were all sat on the sandbags outside of the tents rolling about laughing and holding our sides, struggling to keep them from exploding. It seemed quite extraordinary to be laughing our heads off after what we'd just gone through, but I suppose laughing in the face of adversity was the best leveller. One team had tried a sneaky route by road, planning to hitch a lift for a good few miles then tab up to the RV. The only problem was when they rose from the cover of a roadside dyke to stop the first car, it turned out to be a Land Rover with a BBC crew in it and worse, Eddie and co. in the one behind! Sheer bad luck or fate? Either way, they were up shit creek with no paddle to get out. Their ordeal started a lot sooner than they would have liked and in the end it cost them all the chance to go further on the programme, but still, they could see the funny side of it all.

The BBC missed a brilliant opportunity to film some great footage of the contestants laughing-off all the mishaps, physical pain and mental torture from the previous day's happenings. The rest of the day was spent with most contestants recharging the body's batteries and tending to battered feet. My own were not too bad, just sore pressure points on the soles, but some feet were in a real state. Gary, who was one of the other doctors told us he would be leaving us that night and Dr Mike Stroud would follow the next morning, a decision made by the BBC which didn't go down too well with us. They said there was no further need for them, which wasn't true. They had done a good job looking after our feet and were always on hand for a chat to advise on any medical issues.

The inevitable parade came later and with it a few strong contenders among the dismissals, including Matt, Jonathon and Lee. Lee had had a phenomenal effort on 'Long Drag' the night before after having the worst possible start, which saw him getting lost in the forest just outside the camp. He ran a huge leg of the journey with the 55lb pack and made up for a lot of lost time, but in the process burned most of his body's resources until it finally caved in after the long day and night of Escape and Evasion. Matt, another of the strong contenders hoping to go far, was unfortunately part of the team, which was caught on the roadside. After letting the four members of that group (Anna, Dave, Lee and Matt) go through the interrogation process the DS decided that rules were rules and they all had to go. Matt was absolutely gutted and asked to contest the decision when his name was called out. 'Get on the truck!' was all that Eddie diplomatically offered.

Jonathon had rather surprisingly given up during the early hours of the morning along with Andrew, both believing that everyone else had done so too.

Now we were down to ten and what lay ahead for us tomorrow? There was only Nic and myself left in our tent and for some reason my mind was on overdrive as I struggled to get to sleep.

We'd settled down early at around 8.30pm but I was sure the DS were planning to attack us and see how we'd handle it. Our tent flaps were closed by the staff, adding to my acute paranoia so I lay on top of my sleeping bag with all my kit on, trousers, jacket, boots, the lot, and rifle just inches from my hand. I whispered to Nic before he was in the 'Land of Nod' my plan of action. He must have been saying 'Fuck you mate' under his breath, but he gave me a positive 'Yeah' and 'OK' now and again.

I said 'When it kicks off, you dive behind the sandbags on the left, I'll take the right. Keep me covered, then I'll advance to the pile of bricks near the entrance of the camp, give me some good cover.' When I thought about it, what were we gonna do with deactivated guns? Probably revert back to childhood tactics and just make the gun noises. 'What a stupid prick. What am I thinking about? Get to sleep you idiot.' I eventually took the boots off and jumped into my sleeping bag but was still not totally convinced. We had a good laugh in the morning when we realised our 'house' was still intact.

Camping in January near Braemar.
Character building or just plain crazy?

Checking my bearings. Basic map reading proved to be a big problem for many of the contestants on the programme.

Still looking fresh during a 24 hour charity run.
I managed a distance of 83 miles

Brian & Graham Healy's Spartan training regime provided excellent stamina and endurance workouts

Stick sparring like this had to be abandoned
due to the high injury content

Winter climbing in Arrochar

A moment for reflection during some hard mountain training. Looking down to Loch Nevis

Abseiling down the intimidating 'Inaccessible Pinnacle' on the island of Skye

© Copyright BBC

Emerging from the cool waters of Loch Katrine after the mock river-crossing

© Copyright BBC

Feeling the effects a little, after our first exercise on Ben Lomond. Little did we know that in a few hours' time we would be tackling 'Long Drag'

Senses on full alert during the 'jungle phase'

© Both photographs are the copyright of the BBC

All smiles in 'paradise' after the 'hell', with presenter Dermot O'Leary and ex-SAS Staff Sergeant Eddie Stone

Some of us took up Eddie Stone's offer of a get together in Wales after the programme. Pain forgotten, the smiles returned.

Emerging from the icy waters during the infamous January Tough Guy competition. (Copyright www.toughguy.co.uk)

MY FAMILY AND MY LIFE - - Sue, Cailean and Eilidh

CHAPTER 8

Day 6

Flying High, Sinking Low

We were all getting up sharper in the mornings now and making sure things were in order for the day ahead. Parade was called and ten anxious souls stood, awaiting our next course of action. Eddie let rip. 'You're going skydiving today from 12,000 feet - Freefall!' We all near fell away. This would be a massive bonus for making it this far. No one among us had ever jumped before but I think everyone harboured dreams of doing a jump some day in their lives. I know I certainly did. There were two problems attached to doing it independently. First of all cost can prove very expensive and secondly, there was the question of just having the balls to go and jump! Now it was all there for us which would test each person's nerve to the limit. Eddie explained the procedure then introduced us to the training team, men who had years' of experience with hundreds of jumps between them. It felt reassuring to have such good lads teaching us and passing on their vast amounts of combined knowledge.

It's not every day you throw yourself from a plane and put your life on the line and once the seriousness of the situation sunk in, that was the point when the survival instincts took over. Negative thoughts came faster than a bullet from a gun - 'This ain't normal behaviour, just say now that you're not doing it.'

You just have to override these feelings and tell yourself you are in the best possible hands and that you will have complete trust in the gear that you are using. If all else fails, start flapping hard, or you're gonna be a human pizza. Like I say, I'd always wanted to do a jump but this was beyond my wildest dreams, freefalling with an instructor on either side, and you being the one who would pull the cord at the pre-arranged height. There was fear big time, but also an unbelievable level of excitement. We were split into teams and designated an instructor to whom we would be listening to, intently. The DS gave us all a little treat of sausage and egg rolls and hot coffee. Man that food tasted so good, especially after the past few days.

We trained and trained then trained some more until the procedures were firmly planted in our heads with Stuart, Nic and myself eagerly soaking up all the information available. Then it was into a minibus and a long journey to the east of Scotland and the historic town of St. Andrews where the skydiving club premises were. It would be quite funny being so near to my home city of Dundee, which was only some fifteen miles away, and my family not even aware of it! We were allowed one phone call during our time on the show but I chose not to use it, preferring to switch off completely from my wife and kids. I needed to be focused 100% and thinking of them would just make me emotional.

The sky was a brilliant blue with a few wispy clouds dotted around and a blazing sun beat in through the bus windows, providing us with perfect conditions. Each of us wore the face of a poker player displaying calm on the outside while inside, our heart rates were clocking up more beats-per-minute than we would have liked but still a few laughs were had, more nerves than anything really. We all knew what was expected of us. Carry out the drills smoothly, pull the toggle, parachute opens, land safely on the drop zone, bingo. Any refusal or the instructor having to pull the toggle and you could expect to be dismissed. It was to be a major test under severe stress. On arrival at the Skydiving Club the adrenaline started to kick in big time as we watched other skydivers safely float down to terra firma. We were given more training and signed a document basically saying 'Skydiving is nuts and you are fully responsible for your own decisions'... Cool! As the first man got ready to go up, the rest of us went to the restaurant for some free food which was laid on. Usually when nerves are running high, appetite goes right out of the window but the chance of having bacon rolls, cakes and juice in place of the ration packs proved too good an offer to miss out on.

The toilet was in constant use as the term 'shitting yourself' became very appropriate and at one point Dermot O'Leary, the show's presenter actually interviewed someone on camera after they'd done their business. It gave us all a laugh during the tense situation. Karl was first up and we watched as the three little specks exited the small plane and came plummeting towards Earth at over 100 mph. As their chutes deployed and canopies filled out I breathed a sigh of relief as the trio floated slowly but surely back to the Drop Zone. No problems for Karl (or so it seemed) and when he landed he was as cool and as laid back as ever. 'Well done mate,' we chorused. He later revealed to us that when he was freefalling everything was going fine until he burst through the cloud base and started doing some sightseeing. In those split seconds he'd gone past the pre-planned pulling height of 5,500 feet then thought 'Shit, pull the toggle and release the chute.' The instructor got there before him and pulled at around 5,000 feet. Seconds mean everything when you're up there and any fucking about can cost you your life in a worst case scenario. Stuart was next up and cruising at around 10,500 feet when the decision was made to abort the freefall due to an obtrusive gathering of low cloud.

We were all shattered, Stuart even more so as he was just about ready to leap from the plane. To be pulled back from the brink after going through all the various emotions, must have been a huge letdown for him. Personally, I was absolutely devastated - my big chance ripped away from me by some bloody clouds! The instructors informed us that it was imperative they see the Drop Zone when jumping and so the plug was pulled. I went to the restaurant and stuffed two sausage and egg rolls and another tin of juice down my throat, only to then be told we were changing to static line jumps from 3,500 feet and that Nic, Stuart and myself were going up very shortly.

'Bloody hell, I've just filled my stomach with crap and now it's mixing with surges of adrenaline. That's great … just great!' I felt the urge to be sick but luckily it stayed down. The three of us were taken through the slightly different procedures for a static line jump then before we knew it, we were climbing into the plane with Jim, our instructor, and steadily rising to our height. For a static line jump the parachute is attached to a line which is fixed to a bar in the plane, so that when you jump and count '1000, 2000, 3000, 4000, check canopy,' there should be a large piece of material above your head. If not, you go into your back-up drill and pull the other chute. Jim would be staying in the plane and making sure everything ran smoothly. I checked my altimeter on my wrist. It was almost 3,500 feet. Stuart, who was kneeling in front of me and next to the pilot, received the signal to get ready. Jim opened the door and waited for the pilot to cut the engine, which in turn slowed the plane down sufficiently for the jumper to jump. As the pilot approached the DZ, Stuart got himself positioned and waited those final long seconds for the tap on the back. 'GO,' and he was off, simple as that! The pilot pulled the plane around in a loop and climbed to the spot once more. I was next up, so I shuffled on my knees to the vacated position. On my right hand side I was aware of the huge drop to the ground and by now the adrenaline was on overload. Mr. Negative (that horrible little voice in my head) decided it was time to put on a show. 'Don't do it,' he said. 'Look at the height. You're gonna die!' I gave him a solid right hook and kicked his arse into touch. No way was I gonna bottle this. I got my legs dangling out of the plane and felt the huge explosion of air shooting by, waiting like a 100-metre sprinter waits for the sound of the gun. Tap. 'GO'. I was out and the first thing I felt was the velocity of the air hitting my body. I described it later to Dermot O'Leary as the equivalent of being hit by someone like Mike Tyson (not that I've ever experienced that). Once I checked everything was in order and I definitely had a canopy over my head, I relaxed and took in my surroundings while listening to the instructions coming through my radio via the ground. The sensation of having your body dangling thousands of feet above the ground was awesome. The funny thing was, if my wife and kids had waved from my house I might just have caught a glimpse of them and waved back. I'm just kidding but it wasn't too far away. I landed with a bit of a thud but everything was intact. I was really buzzing at this point. Although we'd changed to a static line rather than freefall, the initial decision to throw yourself from a plane is still the same and requires a massive amount of motivation to override the negative, but probably more realistic and sensible emotions of the mind. Everyone jumped with no refusals or failures. Cass had reason to be particularly pleased with himself as he had managed to successfully overcome his fear of heights. We were all ecstatic! There was quite a bit of hanging around (pardon the pun) during the course of the day so to finish, Eddie gave us a mini-beasting just to keep us on our toes. Then he dropped another of his bombshells. 'You've climbed mountains, you've been interrogated, you've jumped from a plane, now let's see if you can swim!' At first I thought 'OK,' I've had a few visits to the pool and this should tide me over, but I started looking around and realised that most of the contestants were either very good or up to a reasonable standard of swimming. Looking back now, I'd concentrated too much on mountain and running fitness and neglected the water for the simple reason that I didn't think we'd get a major swimming test in the short time the show would run for. In fact I'd only done some 'just in case.'

It was a long drive to Callander High School where the test would take place. Once there, we lined the edge of the pool, decked out not in the latest fashion 'Speedo's', but in combat jackets, trousers, belt kits with water bottles and trainers on our feet. Thankfully, I had the good sense to empty my water bottle which was full, or else I fear I may have been crawling on the bottom of the pool. Cass, who'd brought his new £100 trainers, was adamant he wasn't going in. There was he said, 'No way he was going to wreck them in the water!' We had to talk him out of that idea or he would be 'off the show and on the truck'. Luckily he changed his mind after some serious debate with us and got on with the job in hand. It had been a long day and now late at night, here we were ready for another challenge. 'Right let's do it,' I said quietly, trying to psyche myself up.

One by one Eddie shoved us into what was to become my own personal 'blue Hell' and told us we were being timed. 'No touching the sides, the bottom or cutting corners. Swim all the way round the outer edges of the pool,' he commanded. We all opted for the breaststroke and proceeded on our journey. Each time we passed Eddie, we called out which lap we were on. We were like a load of sheep crammed into a sheep-dip tank battling for a clear piece of water in which to swim. Trainers were connecting with your face, arms, and shoulders while at the back, your legs were being pulled down or smacked (unintentionally) by other peoples' limbs. Everyone was lapping me and the alarm bells started ringing. I heard big Colin (who was an international class tri-athlete) get to ten laps and thought 'Fine, that'll be it.' Eddie growled at him, 'Another ten, move it!'

Strong signs of doubt began to enter my head as I uttered to myself, 'Well it looks like I'm finished then. At least I'd done a parachute jump.' When I reached lap eleven, I was ready to jack it in. I thought, 'What's the point? I'm out of it.' But there's always a point. Something deep inside kept me going. Perhaps it's that same mental strength you dig into when your life is on the line. 'If I'm going out it won't be due to failure.' I told myself 'I'm going to finish this swim if it kills me!' and I meant it. I stopped worrying about the time and concentrated on finishing, every now and then turning onto my back and kind of swimming/floating around. Eddie told me to swim (meaning for me to get off my back) to which I replied 'I am swimming.' I was swallowing heaps of water by now but slowly and surely the number of laps was coming down. Dermot was poolside with the BBC and whispered encouragement as I struggled round. I will never forget his support. Somehow I don't think he was supposed to talk to us but he stuck his neck out to keep me going. Colin had finished first as expected being a really strong swimmer. Shortly afterwards I spotted Cass out of the pool but didn't realise at the time he'd just jacked it in on lap sixteen. He was going really well then apparently 'just got bored' and pulled himself out. None of us could believe it. As more of the contestants were finishing I became aware of the final test they were all doing - a breadth under water.

'How the hell am I gonna manage that in my state?' The rest of the contestants were all offering encouragement as they passed on their way to the changing rooms. I really appreciated that. Now it's only Paul left and myself. Paul was passing me when Eddie said 'Whichever one of you is first, will go through to the next stage.' He (Paul) was already a lap ahead and I'd focused every last cell in my body on just finishing, I couldn't care less who was in the pool or who was saying what anymore. I was completely and utterly working on willpower ... 17 ... 18 ...19. 'Fucking C'mon.' I was shouting, psyching myself up. When I was on my back, only my nose and mouth were above the level of the water and every now and then a pile would flood in, choking me. I clocked Paul poolside when I was on lap twenty so he'd obviously finished. I did not care. I was involved in a personal war with myself. I'd honestly resigned myself to drowning rather than giving up - I was so far gone. I remember finally shouting 'Fuckin' twenty Staff!' in sheer defiance to myself. Eddie stood there towering above me.

'Right, a breadth underwater, move.' I could not stop coughing due to the water I'd swallowed. The pool depth must have gone down a metre when I'd finished! My feet were stealing some much-needed rest on the bottom of the pool but our eagle-eyed Staff Sergeant was on to it. Eddie kept telling me to 'Move it.' I went for it but failed miserably, only reaching about halfway across the pool. At one point I cleared both my nostrils and brought up some mucus from my throat, which I deposited in the pool. Eventually, I took as big a breath as I could without coughing and choking then went again. This time it was now or never as there was nothing left to give. Once my head was under the water I used my family as inspiration and pictured them trapped on a desert island where I had to swim to get to them. I know it sounds corny but the visualization of seeing their faces certainly pulled me through. The feeling of my fingers hitting the other side of the pool was definitely one of the best moments in my life. I felt a great personal achievement. I was cursing and swearing as I paddled back over, then finally I was allowed to pull myself out. Eddie met me and after giving me a quick 'Well done' said 'Right gimme twenty (press-ups) for spitting in the pool.' I actually relished some more hardship and twenty press-ups fitted the bill. I was buzzing. Dermot tried to interview me but I was so high, I was shouting things like 'They'll have to fucking kill me!' I think if I had carried on shouting like that, Eddie would have killed me. It was just sheer emotion. I've never gone that far in life before, but I'm glad I got the opportunity to see right to the bottom of my soul. I thanked everyone for their encouragement when I entered the changing room and then discovered that Cass and Paul had not finished. I still thought I was out though. Back on the bus my emotions went from exhilaratingly high to extremely low, very low, and for the first time I dwelled on my family. Tears ran down my cheeks and dropped to the floor, not for the fact that it was all over for me but just the fact that I'd pulled through the hardest physical and mental test in my life so far. Emotionally, I was drained and physically, I was wasted. Del Boy leaned over and consoled me as a father would his son. Here was a man who had stood toe-to-toe in one of the loneliest places imaginable – the boxing ring and representing his country had fought many of the best international amateur boxers around. This Bristol 'hard man' was a genuinely and incredibly compassionate human being and proved so on many occasions as well as being a bloody good laugh.

    I took heart from his kind words and picked myself up from the depths. 'I might as well go out with a bang,' I thought and launched into Sally Maclennane by the Pogues. Toes were soon tapping on the floor and fingers drummed on the seats as I belted out the lively number. Colin took over the invisible 'mike' next and treated us to some Elvis, which went down well with the assembled little audience. In the space of a few songs I'd gone from being severely down in the dumps to laughing and singing with the rest of the gang. Eddie joined in on the act too after some requests and gave us a song from his army days. Some of the guys had to be shaken from their slumber as the minibus pulled to a halt in the camp. Everyone made straight for their tents and the familiar comfort of the sleeping bags. 'Ah well, I'll be back home in my own comfortable, fresh-smelling bed and snuggled up to my wife tomorrow night.' It seemed a nice thought as I drifted off, exhausted and completely shattered.

CHAPTER 9

Day 7

Then There Were 8

After breakfast we were called onto parade for the dismissals. My heart was pounding as Eddie paced back and forth eyeballing us all. By now we knew what to expect but the waiting was always torture and I remember quite clearly saying to myself that morning, 'Come on Eddie, just put me out of my misery and I'll get off back to my family. First to be called out was Cass. Cass was one of the people I really enjoyed being around although sometimes his clowning caught the watchful eyes of the DS. He was a real personality who always wore a huge smile and had me in stitches on numerous occasions.

Next out, Paul. I waited for my name to be called out but it never came. I couldn't believe it. Luck had played a huge part in my progression on the show, certainly at this point for sure. If Cass hadn't given up in the pool when he was miles ahead of me or if Paul had managed to hold his breath for ten to fifteen seconds, then it would have been me taking the walk to the truck. It just made me realise you should never give up, even when the odds seem highly stacked against you.

The final eight who were left were, Karl, Nic, Andy C, Colin, Stuart, Del Boy, myself and Louise - the last girl, and deservedly still in it. She had competed as well as anyone so far and being of a much smaller frame than the rest of us, had also to work that little bit harder, especially when shouldering the heavy packs. Having reached this far Louise had proved to everyone that she possessed the attributes of determination, resilience and mental toughness and had the mindset to go beyond the pain. Playing international rugby for the Welsh women's team obviously gave her the necessary playing field to toughen her character. She had a petit figure and was quite softly spoken but her body was hardened for battle. I don't think I heard her complain once in all the times I was in her company and she definitely had grounds for complaint.

After Long Drag her feet looked like they'd been left in a fire to cook, they were so badly torn up. She just dug her heels in and got on with whatever was asked of her. 'What's on the psychological menu today?' we all wondered. First of all Eddie told us that we would be together for the next three exercises and there would be no eliminations during that period which was good to know. 'Right, grab four house bricks and put them into your Bergens then jump into one of the Land Rovers. I told myself, 'If we're going back up the hills, I'm ready for it,' but it was to be quite a different challenge today. We were driven to an isolated area of moorland but interestingly, on the way I had noticed a steep rocky crag some miles back and guessed that we were probably going to do some rock climbing and abseiling which would have suited me fine. However, the picture became clearer when peering through a window I spied a Land Rover driving along on what was obviously a purpose-made rough and torn up dirt track, which meandered its way over some steep and challenging ground. Today we were going to take a driving test in the preferred vehicle of the SAS.

Eddie lined us up next to a large catering van, which was stationed in the car park and told us to relax for the time being, even exchanging some light banter with us. A few of the others were very wary of him and still felt rather intimidated by his commanding presence. He certainly did possess a very powerful aura around himself, this being something I've always wondered about how certain people can unknowingly give off this unexplained phenomenon.

The mouth-watering smells that came from the van and passed through our sensitive nostrils had us drooling at the mouth, pining for food. It's not that we were being starved, just that we were burning up so many calories and not really feeling the benefit of the ration packs. 'You can have a coffee or tea, nothing else,' ordered Eddie. It was hard to resist temptation when walking by a table smothered in cooked food, fresh fruit and other exotic goodies, which seemed strategically laid out for our famished benefits, but was in fact there for BBC crew members only - Oh yeah, and Eddie! He took great delight in chomping into some tasty 'real' food while we stood and watched like jealous cats, denied the cream. Our slightly desperate, hunger-induced state was fed with amusement as he spat the words out, 'This is fucking magic. You should try it,' knowing full well we couldn't. As I've stated, some of the contestants really didn't know which way to take him and his dry sense of Scottish humour went down like a lead balloon. I suppose the accent sounds aggressive and confrontational to non-Scots but really, he was a sound guy. I was probably able to relate to him more than the others but that didn't mean we were best of mates. He had a job to do and he did it very well.

A local gentleman who ran the driving courses there briefed us and we listened carefully as he explained the dos and don'ts of handling these all-terrain vehicles. I think the others struggled somewhat with his strong local accent (I must admit, I did a little too) as we tried to digest every piece of information he was giving. Karl, being a policeman, had driven a Land Rover before and told us not to worry but again the adrenaline started to circulate. We were allowed to remove two bricks from our Bergens then jog up to the start point for the test. Stuart was called up first by Eddie and made his way into the driver's seat ready for the test. It took a fair bit of time to complete the course but luckily I was placed second in line and was spared a lengthy wait where nerves can really do some damage. 'Don't mess this up,' I told myself as I sat in the driving seat and listened to the instructor's every word. I took it nice and easy, all the way round, negotiating the many different obstacles which included steep inclines, huge pools of water and a nerve jangling near-vertical drop which we had to throw the vehicle over. Under normal circumstances you may have thought twice, but again you just had to get on with it. It was another good buzz and highly enjoyable experience. I had plenty of time to cook the usual meal of curry, rice and soup on my hexi-burner then get some shut-eye in my sleeping bag as the others went through their test. It was a good feeling being snuggled up in the heather as spots of drizzle came in on the wind. Quite quickly, I drifted off to 'dreamland'. The group gave me a shout when they'd finished and we all made our way back to the car park, only to be met by Eddie who happily announced that we were to have a beasting. This would involve running the course we'd just driven carrying our brick-laden Bergens and rifles.

A good decision made earlier to remove my combat fatigues and change into the waterproof jacket and trousers proved priceless as it meant having dry clothes to change back into after the run. Our feet were soaked again as we waded through the deep-water pools adding to the problems of slight trench foot which some had already encountered previously. Stuart was the first man back from the run and was informed by Eddie that he could have a small meal for himself. He duly cut his 'winnings' into equal portions and shared it out amongst us. It was a great gesture from the youngest person in the group. The lads in the catering van also did us proud as they sneaked the odd plate of leftover chips and pasta our way for us to divide between ourselves. Two or three chips and a couple of swirls of pasta each but it tasted magnificent. Eddie must have been suspicious at the amount of people needing to go to the open-air 'toilet' behind the van. Del Boy was a top performer too as he revealed to us when back on the bus, a sizeable haul of fruit which had managed to attach itself to his 'sticky' fingers. He reminded me of a certain dodgy geezer from the musical 'Oliver'.

We were driven back to camp and thought that that was it for the day but were informed not to cook as we were going for a five-mile run where our meal would be waiting for us. I think that inwardly we all groaned at the thought of a five-mile run with a 35-pound pack on our backs, not to mention the pounding that our feet would take again. 'Right, no complaints, just do it,' the inner-voice was ever present to counter any signs of weakness. We started jogging out of the camp but I was aware of the fact we hadn't been given a grid reference to make for. 'Maybe the DS would be running with us.' We stayed in our two columns of four while passing the farm, then headed up the track to the wooded area where Barry had given us the survival briefing a few days previously. Well he was there again but this time he had a bloody great deer with him, hanging from a tree! We were told to halt. The five-miler was a wind-up. Here before us, was our meal. I laughed to myself as I cast my mind back to my preparation for the programme, reading up on how to gut and skin a rabbit. This was a tad larger than a rabbit and a different proposition altogether. Barry explained the finer details of survival training then demonstrated the art of gutting and skinning the beast. I'm sometimes fussy about what I eat and remember stating on my application form when asked if I needed a special diet for example, vegetarian and I put 'I eat a mainly carbohydrate diet with plenty of pasta and also some chicken.' I felt a right plonker after I sent it off thinking, the 'SAS will just piss themselves laughing at that one!' I could just imagine being in the middle of the jungle and the troop leader saying 'Sorry Gary, we're right out of pasta and tomato sauce, but will boiled snake and termite soup do you?' The saying's true - 'When you're hungry, you'll eat anything.'

Barry plunged the sharp knife into the deer and made a few cuts, letting the guts and shit pour out in front of us. The smell was unbelievable. Barry just kept talking away while cleaning the animal out but even he had to gasp for some fresh air on a few occasions. His expertise was a pleasure to watch and a great learning experience for us all. By now the day's light was fading rapidly and a light rain was beginning to filter through the trees.

Like a scene from the children's programme 'Blue Peter', a large stag was now brought in for us to practice what we had just been taught. Louise, who was a vegetarian I think, volunteered her services and taking the knife from Barry, cut firmly into the throat to bleed the animal. Nic then took over and made the cut in the torso, having the pleasure of clearing out the guts whilst everyone else was designated with different tasks. We were split into new teams of four, ours consisting of Louise, Colin and Del Boy and myself. Those who had done some of the 'dirty' work were allowed to go and choose a spot to construct a shelter for their respective teams to stay in overnight, and also to get a fire going. Myself, Del Boy, Andy and Stuart were left with the task of skinning the two hind legs, and separating them, one for each team. Stuart (who was a fully-fledged vegetarian) mysteriously disappeared to help with his team's shelter building while the three of us struggled in the dark holding torches with our teeth to provide the night's food. The sight of large deer ticks moving around in the fur had us scratching at our own bodies. You had to be extremely careful not to slash your mate's hand as he held the leg steady for you in order to peel the skin away. It took us ages but eventually we retreated to our lodgings for the night and set about making some venison kebabs. The construction of the shelters along with our effectiveness to implement the survival skills was being judged by the DS, (of which two were staying out nearby).

Colin and Louise had made a damn fine den for us to sleep in using a natural pile of fallen pine branches, which boasted a concealed little doorway. The fire was roaring and our faces glowed as we sat, like eager kids away from home on a first scout camp. We cut the meat into chunks and skewered it on branches, holding them over the fire to barbecue. Like I said, I'm a bit fussy when it comes to eating but the meat was exceedingly succulent and very tasty providing a perfect remedy for empty stomachs. Tiredness eventually caught up with us and so the fire was extinguished and one by one we crawled into our home, zipped up our sleeping bags and tried to find the most comfortable position on the bed of twigs and leaves. The odd spot of rain managed to penetrate our roof and splat onto our faces, but it wasn't long before we were all in deep sleep.

CHAPTER 10

Day 8

Red Alert at the Constabulary

I turned over in my warm sleeping bag and forced open my sleep-filled eyes to have a glance at my watch. It was 06.45am and the morning seemed calm and fair enough through an obstructed view of branches and leaves. As I fidgeted about, trying to stretch cramped muscles, the others began stirring and doing likewise. We kept our voices down and asked how each other had slept. Very well it seemed. I pushed my head from the sleeping bag out into the cool air and felt it bite on my nose and ears. The temptation was strong to just 'cosy in again' but it was time to face a new day. As I had been last to enter our 'hide' last night, I was certain that Del Boy had been the one sleeping next to me. Imagine my horror (really it was pleasure) when a beautiful, fresh-faced, blond-haired female surfaced inches from my face. It seemed Del Boy had lost his well-earned flat nose from his years of boxing plus his dark brown hair and unshaven look. We all burst out laughing as Del popped his head out of his bag, which was down at our feet. God knows where the rest of his body was located. He'd been squashed out during the night and had slid away down a hollow, sleeping on an uncomfortable pile of woodland debris. I think he lost the battle to sleep next to Louise, whose pretty features now greeted us with a big smile. The four of us lay there trying to laugh as quietly as we could but it was not easy.

We did up our boots and crawled out of our lair then rekindled the fire, which still had a scattering of warm cinders among its ashes. On Colin's recommendation we boiled up a pot of water and sprinkled pine needles in to it for a rather unorthodox morning brew. It tasted fine (mud and all) and certainly warmed up our chilled bodies. The DS asked if we'd had a comfortable night then took us over to a thing called a hangi, where the other team was also assembled. This ingenious underground oven (which originated in New Zealand) had amazingly cooked our venison throughout the night. The meat was wrapped in leaves, mud and foil and embedded in hot embers to cook away at the bottom of the pit. We were told that nettles make an excellent flavouring if wrapped around the meat. What a breakfast! The venison was still lovely and warm. Soon after, we cleared the area making sure that our fires were out and our environment was returned to its natural look, then we followed the DS for some 'hands on' combat training drills. Both teams were taken through various drills covering how to move effectively, offensively and defensively as a four-man unit, and also how to deal with ambushes and various other scenarios. It was an amazing sight to watch the DS perform the moves so professionally. We tried our best to imitate their precision, speed and all-round awareness and absorb any advice which was being given. I think Louise said she had been in the Cadets when she was younger and this came through in her actions and knowledge of the tasks which we were performing. The rest of our team was well impressed with her. Once we'd had a crash course in patrolling methods it was back down to camp for the next briefing. Eddie told us we were being tested on three separate disciplines covering yesterday's, today's and tomorrow's which was great because it meant no dismissals for the time being. I felt some personal achievement at this point, thinking of some of the strong contenders who'd already gone home and here I was still taking part and loving every minute of it. I think that would have been my biggest disappointment, going home early and missing out on some truly fantastic events, and really just the camaraderie and brilliant fun of it all.

'Today you are going to the firing range to fire a proper rifle,' informed Eddie. 'OK on the minibus, move!' The drive took ages but was helped along by some lovely views of the Firth of Forth on what turned out to be another fine sunny day. Well into the journey though, I realised I had a serious problem on my hands. I began to need a pee desperately, and contemplated asking the driver to stop so that I could nip out and get into some bushes. The trouble was we were in convoy with the BBC, (their guys were driving) and splitting up may have caused a problem finding the destination as we weren't the leading vehicle. So there I sat, going through my own personal Hell in silence, trying desperately to switch off my tortured mind, but my bladder seemed to be at bursting point! At last we pulled into our destination - the Fife Constabulary Headquarters. Being a Sunday afternoon, the car park was fairly empty, and the whole place seemed dead as a ghost town on an old cowboy film. We paused near the main entrance to a large office building with rows and rows of windows facing out towards us. Sitting tight on the minibus and waiting for the all clear to enter the building was no good to me in my 'ready to explode' state. 'Staff, can I go to the toilet, I'm absolutely bursting!' I pleaded. 'Can it wait?' replied Eddie. 'No, not really,' I whimpered. 'Go and use the bushes on the far side of the car park then,' he conceded. Although I was desperate, I was still thinking sharp. 'But there'll be CCTV cameras all over the place.' I said. 'Don't worry,' said Eddie, 'you've got a gun haven't you?' 'OK' I thought. 'I'll have some of that. If Eddie says its OK, then it's bloody OK!' I grabbed my gun, not wanting to risk press-ups for forgetting it, and marched off over the car park. I relieved myself of the torture and nonchalantly strolled back to the minibus where I hopped on. Seconds later, one of the DS from another vehicle came over and inquired, 'Who's the fucking sniper then?' I sensed the seriousness in his voice and owned up. 'It was me Staff. I needed a pee. Eddie OK'd it.'

He said in a half whisper, 'You've just caused a fucking major security alert, wandering over a Police Headquarters car park, dressed in combats and carrying a SLR rifle. They were getting ready to engage the Armed Response Unit for action!' I could sense the laughter finally coming through in his statements and next thing we were all pissing ourselves laughing, but it REALLY could have been a nasty situation. I could just imagine myself being surrounded, in mid-pee, by these fearsome looking characters and having to make those bloody childish gun noises again with my deactivated weapon! Obviously there had been a breakdown in communications with the people in the control room who evidently didn't know we were coming and went into battle stations. The DS joked 'It's OK, there's a few of us here.' With SAS back-up, I think we could have taken on Fife's finest, no problem.

Once inside the building we were all briefed on the safety aspects of being in charge of a lethal weapon then Eddie (who was a trained sniper amongst other things) treated the congregation to a fine display of sharpshooting. Even with ear defenders on, the sound was quite deafening and took a lot of us by surprise. Eddie didn't tell us how well he'd done at the shooting as he may have received 20 press-ups from us for a bad performance. That would have been nice. 'OK Eddie, get down and gimme 20.' I don't think! We were able to watch each other from a viewing room, situated at the rear of the range, but it was impossible to tell how everyone was doing. When it came to my turn, the target seemed a long way off as I struggled to keep the barrel of the rifle steady. It was quite nerve-wracking having Eddie lying close by on your left shoulder, and the cameras just a short distance away, trained on your every move. When you squeezed the trigger, you could feel the sheer power of the weapon as it exploded, propelling the bullet towards the target. We all had ten shots each and by all accounts the DS were not too impressed. Again, not making any excuses, but for the case of our defence we were coming off of the streets as civilians having never fired a gun before in our lives. I'm sure with some steady practice; we could have improved on our performances.

It was a long drawn-out process followed by a long journey back to camp. The minibus pulled in at a garage for a diesel refill and Barry came back with a case of Coke for us. A tin of Coke is usually a small and insignificant soft drink enjoyed by millions worldwide every day, but to us it meant absolute luxury. Later, while passing through a small town on the way home, we approached a junction which had the DS questioning which road to take. Quick as a flash, the DS pulled on the handbrake, leapt from his seat and raced over the busy road where he disappeared into a pub asking for directions. Moments later he came back on the bus with the desired information, then proceeded to tell us he had nearly been lynched by some of the clientele inside. Five o'clock on a quiet Sunday afternoon and he was greeted with 'Hey! Ya English Bastard,' after pleasantly asking which road to take. These drunken bums just didn't know what they were dealing with. Not only that, a busload of hardened volunteers armed with rifles were ready to help out if the need arose but would probably have just been left with the task of loading the broken bodies into ambulances. The funny thing was, that particular man wasn't even English! One of the great qualities had just been demonstrated by the SAS in that instance, and that was self-control. These guys are so professional, they have nothing to prove to anybody, no need to go steaming in thoughtlessly, enhancing the myth which some people have of them.

Once we arrived back at camp we were briefed on our next mission which would consist of a Close Target Recce on an old, disused mansion. We were given grid references on a map and the outline of our mission, then left to plan our own moves. It all sounded very exciting as we re-grouped into our team of Colin, Louise, Del Boy and myself and tried out the gear we had just been handed. Black waistcoats with radios fitted to them, microphone headsets, camouflage cream, night vision goggles plus a drill bit and a tiny camera for inserting into a wall. The plan was this. Under cover of darkness we would be dropped off at the side of Loch Katrine, stealthily make our way down to a shingle beach in a small bay, making contact with our boat patrol. Next, speed off over the loch, rowing in the final stretch creating a minimum amount of noise, and make our way up to the mansion to place the camera in the adjoining wall of the target room. Finally, we were to obtain the information that we required, then get the hell out, just as quietly as we had come in. We were only allowed a window of around two hours, so we would have to shift while at the same time tread very cautiously. The eight of us were taken to the location by minibus where we were told our team would be going first. Our faces and hands were smeared with camouflage cream in an effort to blend in with our surroundings. The cool night bit in as we awaited the order to go, tension building once more while our minds created possible scenarios for the coming next few hours or so. Both teams had been able to view a plan of the building, so it was vitally important to take on the relevant information and general layout of the rooms making sure we didn't have a major balls-up. The order to 'MOVE' came through on our earpieces. We 'Roger'd' the message, and the mission was on. Moving very warily, we covered some flat ground, immediately going into our four man routine as we'd been taught, then made our way steadily through some deep fern and on down towards the bay. Even at this early stage the tense feelings inside had to be controlled as you awaited an attack to materialize at any moment. Our boat was spotted twenty metres from the cover of the fern, swaying to the beat of the light waves on the loch. Cautiously, we approached then a minute or two later we were speeding over the loch at a fair rate of knots. I remember crouching low in the boat thinking, 'It just doesn't get any better than this.' I thought of what I would be doing back home at that particular moment, then smiled to myself as I realized I was not dreaming. This is the kind of stuff you acted out as a boy, playing mock battles with your mates, and now as an adult I was getting to do it for real. Absolutely brilliant!

The engine was cut as the shore loomed in through the darkness and our boat crew prepared to take us in the final fifty metres or so. We slipped into the icy cold water, which reached our thighs and took our breaths for a second, then made our way up to the cover of the trees and bushes. We tried to remember all we had been taught as we crossed the road junction and made our way up to the house, which was brightly lit, making concealment very important. Our plan was going well as we circled the perimeter, creeping slowly through the undergrowth, but I remember growing a little anxious at the time, thinking we were being a little over cautious. The minutes were going by and we still had a job to do once inside. Louise was leading and signaling fairly often to halt and generally, just moving too slowly. On more than one occasion I said under my breath, 'For Fuck's sake, let's crack on a bit quicker. We're gonna run out of time here.'

Speaking to Colin afterwards, he'd felt the same way but for the sake of the team we had approached it diplomatically, and just hinted that we should maybe 'speed things up a little'. The excitement was tremendous as Del Boy and myself entered the old building to insert the camera, while Louise and Colin gave us cover from outside. The first shout of trouble, and we were to abort the mission and make our way out as a unit. The odd cameramen was spotted sneaking about but they were never a distraction, staying well out of our way and letting us get on with the job in hand. It was very dark inside and a mirror situated at the bottom of a rickety old staircase nearly caught me out. My mind was playing tricks thinking it was a corridor, but luckily I trod very gently and realised it was a mirror. The last thing you wanted was a large piece of glass crashing to the floor on a covert mission. To hope the enemy wouldn't hear it would be asking a little too much. Del and I now had the night vision gear switched on and it was he who led the way up the stairs to locate the room in which the camera would be inserted. Mentally, we scoured our minds, trying to remember the plans and making sure we had chosen the correct room. Once we'd found it, Del set to work quietly turning the drill bit by hand to make way for the small camera to fit into. He tried and tried again but couldn't get a picture to display on the monitor. We must have been inside for around twelve to fifteen minutes and at any minute we expected the shit to hit the fan but happily nothing materialized. The monitor had been checked prior to leaving but the damn thing just wasn't taking a game so we decided it was time to clear out, leaving nothing behind as instructed and make our way back to our beach RV. (We only found out later that the wall on which we were working was in fact a few feet thick!)

Silently, we moved down the edge of the mansion driveway and lay under cover near to the road junction, but this time Colin suggested taking an alternative route through some thick trees and bushes in case the 'enemy' had set up a reception party for us. A car parked some distance along the road convinced us it was a good idea. Colin crept out from cover, slithered over the roadside barrier and established himself in good cover on the other side. I was next, and awaited the nod to follow on. Once over I joined him down on the embankment and tried to steady myself behind a tree in order to signal the remaining two over. The problem was, the ground was fairly steep and covered with very dry, broken twigs. As I planted a foot, I lost my balance, stepping on to what sounded like a pile of fireworks going off. I could read Colin's face and lips as he dropped his eyebrows and mimed the words, 'Keep it down.' Each time I tried to correct my footing, I lost it, and more twigs would crackle and snap. The bull in the china shop didn't have a look in! Colin screwed up his face once more, and just fixed me a steely glare. I pleadingly whispered, 'I can't fucking help it.' It seemed like an age before the thrashing stopped, and finally we could bring over Del and Louise. I imagined our escape route would now be smothered with enemy, but nothing came of it so we were able to signal our boat and make good our escape. We sped off over the loch and made the journey back to the starting point, making way for team 2 to begin their mission. We had made it home with time to spare and all the anxiety from earlier on now seemed unjustified. Louise had led us very well indeed. As we communicated with each other, regarding our various roles and how it had all gone, myself and Colin ended up crying tears of laughter as we re-told the episode at the road junction. It was funny now, but in a real situation I would definitely not wear Noddy Holder platform shoes on a mission again! Big Colin admitted that he had not enjoyed this work as much as the other stuff we had been doing but personally, I thought it was fantastic. The other team arrived back at the minibus nearly two hours later, all very chirpy and still buzzing from their mission, where as we by now, were shivering our arses off, trying to stop ourselves from becoming hypothermic. The long wait in wet clothes had meant a drop in our core temperatures, prompting continued bouts of uncontrollable shivering. Our responses to their highly excitable attempts at conversation must have been downright rude to say the least, but 'Fuck it,' we were freezing!

CHAPTER 11

Day 9

A Child for A Day Again

Another morning dawned and still we had no dismissals. We didn't know it at the moment, but today was going to be a cracker, a real taste of some SAS close combat work, albeit a very small taste. These guys learn so many skills and accumulate such a vast amount of knowledge and 'hands on' experience that for us, as a group of raw civilians from the streets, to be trained by them was just truly awesome. The whole mood of the contestants by now was much more relaxed than the earlier, more high impact days. We were now moving into the more skilful element of the course and there were signs beginning to show that one or two people were either getting homesick, or had just had enough of the constant wearing down of the mental muscles. Some of the lads had said that if they were to be binned at this stage, they were not too bothered, as they had been given the opportunity to do a parachute jump. I suppose it was fair comment, but personally, I was feeling stronger by the day and did not want to miss out on a single thing. After a lovely breakfast of bacon, fried eggs, beans, sausages, a mug of hot tea and some toast with lashings of raspberry jam ... 'No snap out of it!' I don't have to tell you what we were having by now, but it was nice to daydream for a few seconds.

We were taken to another disused house not too far from camp, which we would be using for close quarter battle drills. The house itself was not derelict, but a fairly new building which was awaiting some new occupants to come along and make it a warm, welcoming home once more. It seemed a shame for us to be charging around in such a nice setting, but there was a job for us to do and even nice settings can be home to some dark characters. Our job or training today would be to weed them out. We were given gas masks to wear, which were awkward to operate in. The secret of using these clumsy devices was not to panic and trust that enough oxygen was getting into your lungs - not easy when you are rushing from room to room, trying to locate the enemy and deal with heavy fire coming back at you. Add some shouting to our old friend, 'adrenaline' and the fact that we were playing for real, then you start to get a picture of the exciting drama which we were involved in. We also wore ear defenders which caused a problem for communication with each other. Our every move had to be made by signal or physical contact.

The BBC had hired a couple of guys to come in and supply exact replica weapons which fired high velocity pellets, creating an air of reality for the drills. Somehow I couldn't see them letting us loose with live ammo. One can only imagine the scene of utter carnage the BBC would have had on their hands as we 'let rip' at each other. With our newly obtained weapons in our hands, everyone set to having some practice on nearby trees, fence posts and other stationery objects which we now viewed as enemy. The SA80 rifles could be set to single shot or rapid burst. Guess which one everybody had on? We all had our 'Al Capone' heads on as bursts of rapid fire disrupted the calm peace of our surroundings. I think all the wildlife in the area wisely buggered off when they saw the hardware being handed out to our little band of would-be SAS troopers.

The DS demonstrated the use of a 'flashbang' and instructed us on the importance of this valuable weapon when clearing rooms or confined areas. These oversized fireworks would be lobbed into a room, given time to explode thus creating panic and confusion, then followed up by a wave of sheer aggression and firepower. Both teams practiced over and over, alternating between hunter and hunted. The DS would sometimes play the part of a hostage with the other team defending the target room and our team seeking to systematically clear the house and take out the hostage.

Poised like springs, we waited outside the main front door, adrenaline pumping through our bodies as we focused our eyes on the DS, awaiting the call to 'Go'. We mixed up the positions in our four-man team giving everyone the chance to experience the difference in roles. Mistakes were pointed out to us often, as the Staff assessed our performances. One of the classics being two men wedged in a doorway at once. Not the kind of thing you would want on a real job. We were all enjoying the training immensely and having a few laughs into the bargain, when on one occasion Del's eagerness and over-zealous behaviour created some mayhem. He proceeded to burst into the target room and 'let go' with some heavy fire, taking out the enemy, the hostage and two of our team as he sprayed the whole area in an arc of death. All I can say is 'Thank God they were pellets.'

Time passed into the afternoon as our house training came to a close and a fresh challenge lay literally just around the corner. Lined up in two columns of four, we were ordered to place our gas masks on our faces then run the short distance up to the vicinity of the forest. It was one of the hardest little runs I've ever taken part in. The limited oxygen being supplied to pumping lungs seemed woefully inadequate as we eventually came to a halt. Our suffering was prolonged as we awaited the order to remove the masks. Lungful's of fresh air were greedily sucked in when we did finally receive the order to 'Remove'. The DS gave us all something to think about when he said, 'Try that in a live situation with a heavy pack, spare ammo and a weapon.' I could only imagine how hard that must be, gauging it against what we had just done.

We were then told to relax while our next task was set up. Eddie turned the heat up a little when he shouted, 'Gary, you are going first.' I asked myself what it could be, but tried to concentrate on staying calm and relaxed as the butterflies fluttered around in my stomach. Each time I was called to 'go', somebody or something wasn't ready and my mind became a rollercoaster of emotions. Meanwhile, a BBC crew interviewed us one by one, asking for our thoughts and views on everything we had taken part in so far and were we enjoying it. They also wanted to know who we reckoned was the strongest contender to win the whole course. Karl was still the name on everyone's lips, mine included, and also Colin whom I thought had performed very steadily. There was one small thing at the back of my mind though, which told me Karl's heart or enthusiasm may be faltering and that small thing was his motivation. He just didn't seem fired up any more. I know he was in a fair bit of pain from one of his feet - a large area of skin missing from the sole, but never once did he complain about it although it must have been wearing him down mentally.

When asked how important it was for myself to progress to the last day, I answered that it wasn't that important at all, but what I really meant to say was the competitive hunger to beat everyone else was not the issue. In all honesty I never began the programme with the attitude, 'Sod the rest' at all, and I don't think any of the others did or at least I wasn't aware of it. Sure it would be great to win the show, but always first and foremost, the battle was with my own mind to see how far I could possibly go and if that meant at the end I was the winner, then I would be over the moon. Immediately after I'd done the interview, I regretted what I had said as it must have sounded like I didn't really care if I stayed on the show, but nothing could be further from the truth, and I mean NOTHING!

It was going to be sad for the ones being dismissed, especially as we had bonded really well over the last few days and had gotten to know each other on a more personal level with some good laughs thrown in there as well. I imagine that's not the case on a proper selection with the candidates concentrating on their own performance and not devoting much time, if any, getting to know the others. It was different for us coming from civilian life and no one really wanted to stand out too much as a loner, also we did things in teams on the latter stages whereas SAS candidates would probably be fending for themselves.

Our extended wait produced a hilarious moment as the BBC conducted their on-going interviews. Two horses that were happily chewing grass in the same field as us suddenly took an interest in the proceedings, (possibly looking for a walk-on part in the show) and boldly forced themselves into our company. Instantly, they took a liking to Karl who was feeding them the crap biscuits from his ration pack. Most of our food was fine, or at least edible but these certain biscuits tasted like they had been dipped in paraffin then flavoured with methylated spirits. They obviously hit the right taste buds with this pair of nags as they constantly pestered Karl, even attempting to chew his belt kit. As the interviews were taking place only a short distance away, any noise from the background would be picked up on camera. For some strange reason, the build up of dangerous gases in our stomachs (due to the constant curry diet) decided it was time to leave via our arses and everyone started to drop some serious 'bombs'. Every so often the heads would turn from the camera crew and whisper to us to keep the noise down as we giggled away like a bunch of school kids. Then one of the horses joined in on the act and let off a thunderclap of its own! We all just exploded into laughter. It was a case of 'Take 2' on that particular interview as even the Beeb guys broke their self-discipline.

Finally my name was called once more and the serious business was on. The guys wished me good luck as I doubled over to the edge of a wooded area where the DS was standing. One of the pellet-firing rifles was given to me along with a pair of protective goggles then I was wired up with a small mike by the BBC for the purpose of monitoring my reactions. The DS explained what was required. This was to be the mock Jungle Phase section as we followed a track through the woods, firing on targets as they appeared while keeping an eye out for booby traps. Explosions would also be set off en-route to test our nerve. Staff told me I was being timed, but not to worry and just to move steadily and confidently with plenty of diving for cover and good positioning in order to take out enemy targets. I drew in a deep breath then psyched myself up saying, 'Come on Robertson, a good performance here might just be enough to see you through boy. Let's do it!'

The DS shadowed me as I embarked on my journey through the forest, the old adrenaline on overload once more. 'Control it', I thought as I trod warily over the muddy, worn track, anticipating any slight movements in order to take action. Bang! 'Fuckin' hell, that was loud,' I said in my mind as turf and debris flew around, although I wasn't unsteadied by it. As the targets popped up, I dived into the mud or consolidated a good position, then took aim and let off a round. I felt I'd done reasonably well as the DS told me it was over and to make my way back down the track to camp. I had now completed the three disciplines which we were being tested on (the Land Rover test, the Rifle Range and the Jungle Phase) and could only hope I had done enough. I had certainly tried my best.

I chewed on a dextrose sweet as I made my way smartly back to base, taking in the magnificent scenery on what was another glorious, sunny afternoon. In no time at all, the contents of my ration pack were emptied and poured into the trusty mess tin to be mixed with water and produce some sustenance for my extremely empty belly. I sat perched on a sandbag, all alone in the deserted camp with just my own thoughts for company. Some time elapsed before the second person (Stuart) arrived and told me to get back up to the farm for a slap up feed compliments of the catering van.

'Eddie must be going soft' I thought. I had just had a good scoff but the thought of some real food had me doing somersaults. I was surprised to find most of the others had completed their test in the 'jungle' and were now enjoying a very unexpected but welcome meal. We were allowed to have whatever we wanted from the menu, so I opted for the potato and leek pie with heaps of chips and a desert of jam pudding and hot custard. It really was magnificent, one of the best meals which I have devoured in my life! The fact that I had already had a full feed a short time ago didn't make the slightest bit of difference as I wolfed the lot down. All except Colin had now joined us and what a picture their faces told as they pulled up a seat at the table and eyed their unexpected prize of proper food in disbelief. This was a real bonus and a nice gesture. While we ate, some of the lads said they didn't think they had performed the task too well and stated that they had not dived about enough. Again, I suspected some of the early enthusiasm might have gone in a few of them, but only the SAS guys would know and decide our fate.

Darkness was very nearly upon us when Colin finally joined the company pumped up and buzzing from his experience. God knows how he managed to see the targets in the fading light. He had openly admitted to disagreeing with government policies worldwide on warring with other nations, but sometimes the necessity arises and action has to be taken and the mood Colin was in right now, he was ready to kick some serious ass!

After a good round of banter, we all made our way back to camp and holed ourselves up in a tent to await the agony of the final dismissals. On reflection, the day had involved tasks which were serious in content, but had taken me back to my days as a wee boy playing soldiers in derelict houses and fields with all the excitement and innocent fun with which that brought. How lucky I was to find myself now 'playing' as an adult.

We lay on the camp beds relaxing under the canvas roof and began sharing all the fantastic laughs and experiences we had endured on our adventure. Tears ran down our cheeks as we went into hysterics when someone recalled some other funny incident or mishap. Suddenly the hilarity ceased as the tent flap swung open and the dark figure of one of the DS, silhouetted against the bright spotlights of the camp.

'Robertson, come with me,' he said, matter-of-factly. 'I want you to sing that song you sung the other night!' 'Oh shit' I thought. 'If I'd had a good few malt whiskies, then yes, no problem, but now, here, in front of all the contestants, DS and camera crew.' A few nights back I'd laughed at Nic for getting 20 press-ups during a light-hearted moment with the DS and quick as a flash the DS had said 'OK Robertson, sing a song.' I instantly stopped laughing and hurriedly searched in my mind for an appropriate song. I'd opened with the first few lines from Killiecrankie - a traditional Scottish folk song when I was abruptly told to 'Shut it.' 'Yes Staff,' I replied like a wee mouse. Now, at present my bottle was being tested in a different way from all my other escapades and I did not want to crack, not at this point. Fuck it. I stood there in the middle of the camp, gun in hand and burst into song, three verses and the chorus. At the end, I was shaking like a leaf, but

I'd done it, and it felt bloody good, even though a trained singer would probably have had me strung up.

Shortly afterwards, we were all lined up for the final dismissals. Who goes? Who stays? My heart felt like it was bursting out of my chest, the beats increasing rapidly as the tension mounted. Eddie paced back and forth once more, eyes piercing, chest out, shoulders pulled back. 'Karl Webster. On the truck.' That was a shock to myself, and I would say the others too, but the DS had decided otherwise. Stuart Crispin and Andy Collins (both members of the London Fire Brigade) followed, as did Del Boy, the boxer from Bristol. Great guys, each and every one, they really were.

For those of us left the worry and anxiety now turned itself into a great sense of achievement and delight with each of us openly admitting that we expected to be ordered onto the truck. I could not believe I had made it this far when I considered the calibre of fellow contestants way back at the start, but I must have been doing something right. Originally, getting a few days participation and not going home first was my goal and anything after would be a bonus, taking each day at a time. Nic, Louise, Colin and myself congratulated each other on making it through while at the same time feeling for the lads who had just left. We had been through a lot together but now we had to concentrate and focus our minds on tomorrow, the last day - or so we thought.

One contestant who was still there may come as a surprise, yes that slight, quiet spoken girl called Louise. People may say that it was a BBC decision in order to make for better telly. A kind of 'We'd better have a girl in the last four' to make sure there was still some female input, but I believe Louise was still there purely on merit as the BBC had no say in who stayed or who went anyway. She was a tough girl. Nic was still there also. I looked back on the day when he had produced his toiletry kit in our tent and remember having a light-hearted dig at him for being a soft boy, but a soft boy he certainly was not! Colin - well Colin was just Colin, steady and strong throughout! The four of us slept in the tent that Nic and I had been sharing and I guess we all must have gone to sleep with similar dreams and hopes for the coming day.

CHAPTER 12

Day 10

The Final Assault

The four of us were up sharp and cooking our breakfast for what was to be the last time. It was strange how those of us who were left now seemed so programmed and organised, a far cry from the shambles, which had been woken in the early hours of the first morning.

One thing we had been very lucky with throughout the duration of the course was the fantastic weather and this morning proved no exception. The weather in these parts can be damn miserable at times even in the summer and I must confess, deep down, I had hoped for terrible conditions to make it as tough as possible. There was absolutely no need. Apart from Mother Nature lending a helping hand on the Escape and Evasion exercise, the course had proved to be immensely tough with a capital 'T'. I had a quiet laugh to myself as I recalled one of the contestant's remarks on the night that we arrived in the camp. Eddie had been passing every volunteer and making a comment concerning the content of their application or video for the programme, when one smart arse quoted, 'I don't think it will be hard enough! Needless to say, it had proven to be too tough for him and he did not make it to the final day. Each of us when being interviewed admitted that we were extremely happy to have made it this far and all wished each other 'Good Luck' for the final outcome.

As I wandered down to the little stream at the back of the camp to wash my dirty mess tins, I was already thinking 'I'm gonna really miss this.' Quite simply, I did not want this adventure to end. Last night had been hard when our four companions were dismissed but sentimental feelings could wait. The show had to go on and staying focused was going to be the key for getting through the final test.

Eddie called us onto parade for a quick briefing, congratulating all of us on getting this far and outlining the task, which lay ahead of us tonight. The rest of the day was spent training, going over and over the last mission until we had a clear plan in our heads. Eddie also commented on how far we had come from day one, and how much we were starting to think and act like soldiers. We were probably a long way from the finished article, never mind Special Forces, but the enthusiasm, excitement and willingness to learn was very much in evidence in the contestants who had managed to survive.

In reality, today was supposed to be the final day, but it would be tomorrow before we would all be home as filming had run over, slightly. Colin was due back at his work tomorrow and had to make a hasty phone call to extend his 'holiday'. I dread to think what the BBC would have done if one or all of us had to be home due to work commitments or any other business. Personally, I was staying in that camp until they dragged me out kicking and screaming. I gave my wife Sue a very brief call to say everything was going well and that I would be here for another day yet. She was over the moon to hear from me. After hearing her voice I began feeling quite emotional (the very reason I had not phoned before) and when I came out of the building Eddie noticed this and called me a 'Big Jessie', but having a strong family unit means more to me than anything.

As evening approached, we were given our final briefing from the DS, and we in turn explained our proposed plan. We knew the lay of the land now from our previous recce mission and first off, (after being inserted under cover of darkness from the speedboat) we would have to take care of a sentry whom we were told would be patrolling the pier. Next, we would move to the target building and await the order to 'Go' from HQ, storm the house, clearing rooms as we went, and finally extract 'Barkan' the war criminal, who was wanted for atrocities. Barkan was to be played by Graham Cooper, the producer of the programme, who'd bravely put himself forward to face our aggressive onslaught. Tonight there would be no messing about.

We were issued once more with our gear, the only difference being this time that the pellets had tracers in amongst them, which would look cool at night when we let off a burst or two should the need arise. This time, I think the need was going to 'arise' big time and the dummy flashbangs we had would be simulated in set-up explosions. One thing was for certain - it was going to be extremely noisy when it all kicked off and we all agreed the ear defenders would be a welcome addition.

Adding to the realism of it all, we heard that the DS were going to be defending Barkan but where they would be placed - we knew not. Once more we smeared the cam cream onto our faces and began mentally preparing for the task ahead. The sun was sinking in the sky as our Land Rover careered around the sharp bends on the single-track road, which skirted the edges of Loch Katrine. The four of us were dropped off with a BBC photographer and whilst we all waited, had a majestic view of the loch and surrounding hills, which were being 'fired' by the last rays of light. Bright colours turned to grey, then slowly to black as night took a grip, and the warm temperatures of the past day began to dip. We thought the BBC would have everything in place, ready to rock and roll as soon as darkness was upon us but frustratingly, the night dragged on and on. A briefing was called by the BBC to make sure everyone was aware of the dangers involved with explosives going off and really, just a general call for safety from everyone. We just wanted to get on with the job, just get in there, do the business then relax at the end of it all - but still we waited. As we hung around in the Land Rover trying desperately to stay focused and switched on for the coming mission, a camera crew appeared wishing to conduct some interviews with us, and I must admit by now our patience was being strongly tested and we were all fairly pissed off. I'm sure it was the only time during the whole filming of the programme where nobody really wanted to speak to the cameras. It was just very bad timing as the four of us by now were tired, agitated and very grumpy due to the large build up of adrenaline in our bodies and nowhere to unleash it. 'What the hell's the hold up?' we asked each other as long minutes turned to even longer hours. I'm sure the BBC wanted everything to be spot on, but it was still frustrating all the same.

Nic, Louise, Colin and myself were now beginning to doze off. It was all a bit of a come down, a huge anti-climax really, after the initial adrenaline rush we had experienced when heading up to the lochside. We all agreed, however grumpy and annoyed we had become, that once we received the call sign to go, we would do our absolute best. We owed it to Barry, Eddie and the DS who had placed their faith in picking us to do the last mission, and of course, we owed it to ourselves having come so far. All that training though was now about to be severely tested.

We all jumped as our radios crackled into life. It was the signal we had been waiting for, and instantly the body was given a fresh supply of adrenaline, gearing us up for some action. 'This is it folks, let's do it for Barry and the lads,' we all choroused. We left the safety of the Land Rover and trod very warily once more, just as we had done on the Recce mission and made our way down to our RV with the boat. I suppose our minds were on overtime again, but the thought of an all-out gunfight on the beach seemed very real to us. We just did not know what lay ahead of us and that was probably the most exciting bit of all. Everything physically and mentally needed to be in top working order. It is easy looking back now knowing that the chance of an attack at an early stage was just about nil as the SAS would have had to be in two places at the same time. I am sure even those guys could not pull that one off, but who knows? Our boat scudded off over the loch once more and delivered us near to the vicinity of the pier, where our first objective, the sentry, could be seen patrolling along the walkway.

The freezing cold water squelching in our boots sounded to us like a tsunami festival crashing around in an ocean, with every single move seemingly amplified to an unacceptable level. It's amazing how the body's senses experience a heightened awareness when operating in a highly tense situation. We hugged the soft sand by the water's edge and crept mouse-like to the cover of a boathouse, situated at the end of the pier. Standing on the pier were a few spotlights making the importance of cover, the number one priority. We paused, our hearts racing as we waited for the right moment to pounce. The last thing we wanted was a major balls-up right at the start of our operation.

Earlier in the day, we had gone over the plan nominating certain individuals for different tasks so that everyone in the patrol had the opportunity for some action, but in reality, it would be a rolling, changing outfit hoping to deal with whatever was thrown at us. Colin was the man selected for the execution of the sentry and led us round the corner of the boathouse wall to take up a position at the bottom of the staircase. Twelve feet above, the sound of heavy boots clumping on the broad beams of wood overrode the constant background noise of gentle waves softly lapping the shore. The target began moving away from our concealed position and I'm thinking, 'Go for it Col … Take the bastard out now!' These fractions of seconds seemed to last for ages as we anticipated Colin's rifle exploding into action. 'Sod it,' I took aim on the sentry's back, (who was about twenty feet away now) and let rip with a short, sharp deadly burst. He slumped to the ground in a heap. The feeling was quite surreal, much like a dream but reality soon kicked in again and I thought, 'Hey, I've just killed someone.' Of course, it was all an act although it did seem real enough to warrant feelings for a fellow human being. The thought quickly vanished as we mounted the stairs, regrouped and then made our way smartly off the walkway, so far so good. We had to move sharp as we were sitting ducks at that point, appearing as four nicely illuminated targets for a machine gunner or sniper. This time on the approach to the house, we moved more positively, but always staying alert in preparation for a possible attack. We had made it safely to the gable end of the building and crouched low covering all angles as we awaited the call sign to 'Go'. A gentle tap on the shoulder from Nic alerted me to drop my gas mask over my face and put on the ear defenders in readiness for entry to the house. We held the position for a long period of time which broke the whole rhythm and momentum of the team. I was kneeling on one leg, my eyes glued down the barrel of the gun, not daring to let them wander astray from the spot I was covering. At any moment I imagined an attacker peering round the opposite corner of the building where my sights were trained. I'd let them have it. Other thoughts started filling my head, things which were totally irrelevant and each time I had to erase them from my mind and concentrate one hundred percent on our next moves.

The longer the situation stayed static, the more the negative thoughts came flooding in, 'What the bloody hell is going on. They have had all day to get this operation running smoothly.' It was very frustrating but worth the wait when the voice came through on the earpiece. 'Go!Go!Go!' The excitement was unbelievable as our bodies went into attack mode once more. We tried to keep our formation tight as we moved at pace along the wall, which ran in an L shape past a door, the same door which we had entered previously on the recce and finally took up position on either side of the target entrance door. I was covering our rear and running backwards at the same time while the others moved a little quicker than I would have liked and were already preparing to enter as I caught up. I thought we would maybe spend a second or two composing ourselves before we charged in but the excitement had taken over and we probably seemed a bit ragged going in. A flashbang was chucked in and exploded with a massive bang, which heralded our arrival. There was no turning back now! On entering the hallway we were taken completely by surprise as a heavy burst of machine gun fire poured down on us from the top of a stairway to our left. The ferocity and noise of the attack was totally unexpected, as we'd imagined a straightforward easy mission where WE would be the aggressors; A simple case of in, get the job done and out, just like the DS had hinted at. I guess we'd lowered our guard a little.

Once we had gathered our senses and briefly subdued the gunman upstairs, we turned our attentions to the doorway immediately to our right, while at the same time covering the lower hallway to our left. The hallway was well lit and through the restricted vision of the gas mask, I remember noticing the interior of the house being very old-fashioned in design. I don't know why I was thinking about décor. It seemed a rather strange thought to have in such a bizarre situation. The place had probably been empty for years but for this one night, it was transformed into a mini battleground where you really got the feeling that your life was on the line. The sound of explosions and gunfire vibrated through our ear defenders and bounced from wall to wall, the noise being amplified in the close confines of the house. We were certainly playing this for real.

We hesitated at this first door like a group of kids does when daring each other to go into a haunted house, as we had that awful feeling of something nasty lurking inside, waiting for us. There was a very real danger of the whole episode just passing you by and with this in mind it became vitally important to stay alert and ready to react to the situations as they arose.

'Stay switched on you bastard,' I told myself as I locked my eyes onto the door, and watched as a team member turned the handle and partly opened it. Would this room be empty or not? I was soon to find out. Incredibly, none of us thought to throw a flashbang in before we assaulted the room. I moved forward a little slower than I would have liked as a huge surge of adrenaline raced through my body, anticipating what lay in wait behind the door. I gave it a healthy boot to open quicker, while at the same time I placed my finger onto the trigger of my rifle in readiness. The large room exploded into mayhem as a lone 'terrorist' opened up, taking the fight to us immediately. Reaction time plays a huge part in a situation like this where any indecision could prove fatal.

My trigger finger squeezed into action homing straight in on this person in front of me who I saw only as a terrorist - an aggressive, gun-wielding threat to my life. By now our No 2 (Louise) was also in on the fight, laying down some lead (or should I say pellets) into our target's body, just to make sure. At this point, like in any fight (although thankfully, I have never been in a gun battle) sheer aggression kicks in once the fight is initiated and the sense of focus seems to increase to an otherwise unreachable level.

I should also point out that I took out a cameraman who was on the far-side wall, just minding his own business and getting on with his job. He looked suspiciously like a terrorist to me in all the excitement! On a serious note, shooting a 'friendly' in a real situation would be unthinkable. It was a real reminder to myself just how professional and controlled the SAS guys really are as they practice with live ammunition all the time. Louise and myself screamed 'Clear, Go' and moved along the hallway to the next room while Colin and Nic continued to be harassed by the gunman at the top of the stairs. I turned the handle and gave Louise the pleasure of entering first, like any good gentleman should and again we forgot to initiate the entry with a flashbang. This room was slightly smaller than the previous one but once more it provided us with a contact from an enemy figure that was backed into an alcove at the far end of the room. Louise sprayed him with death and I made sure with a burst of my own. During all the action, we were desperately trying to remember our training drills and cover each other. With the ground floor now cleared, it was time to move up the stairway. Our 'friend' reappeared once more on the upper landing and continued to cause us problems until his weapon conveniently jammed, which allowed us to seize the initiative. We snaked up staying as close to each other as possible, weapons poised, ready for another onslaught. Colin lobbed a flashbang up onto the landing, which exploded with a terrific CRACK and temporarily forced the terrorist into retreat, giving us the upper hand for a moment as we checked out a little dead end corridor for more enemy. First room upstairs, 'Is this the one where all hell is gonna break loose?' Louise and myself went in. It was another all clear. One room left. 'Here we go folks.' Colin and Nic burst into the final fury, backed up by Louise. I think it must have been exciting for Graham who was playing Barkan, hearing this tidal wave of aggression and firepower grow closer and closer threatening his safety. The enemy was thoroughly wiped out while Barkan received the rough treatment.

There was no messing about, producer or not he was told in no uncertain terms to do exactly as we ordered. It was quite tempting to give him a good doing, especially in the adrenaline-charged mood we were in but that would not have been a wise move at all as we all had to get home the next day when the war was over.

'Okay, let's get the fuck outta here,' I said to myself, 'it's time to shift – fast!' Three of us were screaming orders and obscenities at Barkan while Louise covered the doorway. Colin finally grabbed Barkan and forced his head down roughly then dragged him from the room, aided by the rest of us then we all scrambled down the staircase and out into the courtyard. We rendezvoused back at the corner of the gable end where we had originated the attack and paused for a few moments while we gathered our sanity. The relief from lifting the gas masks off of our faces was immense. My body perspired profusely from the exertions of our efforts in what was probably a very short, but incredibly explosive (to put it mildly) period of time. We did not linger in case of any follow-ups, which we were expecting, and were off down the driveway like a gang of Linford Christie's dragging poor Barkan with us. We made it safely to the beach and radioed our boat to extract us ASAP.

The engines from the launch roared into action way out in the Loch and sped across the murky, black depths, whipping up masses of frothy foam. 'C'mon, hurry up. We're gonna be caught here,' I thought, anxiously willing the boat in. We were a bit too spread out as a team with Colin and his hostage already out in the waiting boat. Suddenly, two figures appeared way over on the right, running along the pier under the glare of the spotlights. 'Oh, Oh, here we go again!'

Louise and me were still on the beach and so nearest to the enemy and let rip with a thunderous volley, the tracers cutting a path through the night sky, all the way to their illuminated targets. Nic, who was getting ready to wade out to the boat, decided to give us some back-up. Actually, I think he just had too much ammo left in his magazine and needed to use some of it up, but what the hell!

We started advancing on the enemy, firing at will, while Colin who was perched on the boat with our hostage was screaming at us to get our arses aboard, pronto. 'Aye, Aye Cap'n. This is bloody great,' I thought, a huge grin stretched over the length of my face, but all good things must end sometime. I'm sure my reaction may have been somewhat different had the bullets been of the 'real' variety, of course that's if I was lucky enough to be alive to have any reactions. The three of us thought we were at Rorke's Drift or Custer's Last Stand, but eventually and somewhat reluctantly we waded into the freezing cold loch and pulled ourselves into the boat. We had paid for having a 'stand off' on the beach though as the boat had floated further away from the shore by the time we'd headed out to it, and now Nic and myself were rewarded with iced bollocks, while Louise had iced something different. Mission accomplished! We were absolutely buzzing and talked excitedly on how it had all gone, with everyone sharing their own personal feelings and experiences on how they had felt during the different stages of the mission. We all congratulated each other and became friends with Barkan once more who was none the worse for wear, just a little wet, then it was back onto the beach for some interviews with the BBC. The story did not end there though.

In the only incident of its kind, we were asked to recreate the 'Battle on the beach' scene as the BBC had not captured it properly. All through the course, everything was filmed as it had happened, nothing at all was put on and I mean nothing except for this little blip in the proceedings. We hung about for ages, freezing our butts' off as the camera crew dithered, then finally we got down to shooting the last scene again. Louise was very nearly hypothermic by now and the rest of us weren't that far behind as we started to shiver uncontrollably in our soaking wet gear. When the cameras had shot what they needed, we shuffled up to the road to fetch a lift back to the farm. Barry Davies was coming down the driveway from the 'target house' where all the drama had unfolded and we were eager to quiz him on his thoughts of how we had performed. When asked, he replied unemotionally 'That was average.' 'Well thank you Barry, thanks a lot.'

We had just busted our arses off doing our absolute best for these guys (SAS), especially them, and were a little taken aback by his cold-seeming words. There were no, and would never be any hard feelings though. It had been a very long day and night, and now we were well into the wee small hours. It was only natural for people (and that included ourselves) to get slightly agitated and snippy with each other and to be honest, everyone was in need of a damn good rest. Barry himself shook all our hands before leaving straight away for another engagement. It was a great privilege to share the time we had with him.

We also spoke to Eddie and a couple of the DS who informed us that we had done 'alright' for a first time effort. Again, in all honesty, we had tried our very best and could be quietly pleased with the outcome. Never again would the evil Barkan create such terror amongst the ordinary citizenry of his country, certainly not while we were around anyway. The whole mission was brilliant fun but at the same time serious in nature, giving us a very high feeling of reality plus a very small taste of what it's like to be in a situation like that. Thank God the enemy were firing blanks, (no offence intended lads). One of the guns that were used by the enemy was an old World War II sub-machine gun, which made a hell of a racket when fired.

Controlling the fear and having total confidence in your own and your patrol's ability are probably the major factors when dealing with the 'real', and also the meticulous planning which is needed beforehand in order for the mission to go like clockwork. If the unexpected should happen, adapt, and deal with it. We didn't have real bullets coming our way, which I suppose, would really turn the fear levels up, but for that short period in our lives we had experienced in some small way a taste of Close Quarter Combat.

Ultimately now, the small matter of picking the final winner would be upon us within hours but that could wait for now. We had worked as a team and worked very well. Now it was time to wind down and rest both physically and mentally and try to get a few hours' sleep. With the heating turned on full blast in the Land Rover, we made our way back to the farm and were shown into our luxury accommodation for the remaining hours of darkness. Tough to the end, there was to be no upmarket 5-star hotel with mountains of exquisite food or gallons of fine wines from around the globe. The door of the bunkhouse creaked open to reveal a cold, dark room, which we entered into and with some difficulty we began faking the wood-panelled wall for a light switch. A BBC guy hung around for a few minutes (fortunately not with his camera) and made sure we got settled in. A dozen bunk beds or so dominated the far end of the room complete with a large pile of sleeping bags and at the opposite end there was 'heaven' in the form of a shower cubicle. The thought of having a proper wash under a steady jet of warm water seemed too good to be true. A small convector heater was switched on and spluttered into action giving a tiny hint of heat to the spacious room. We were asked if we would like a drink and something to eat. 'You bet! I could murder a Guinness,' I said enthusiastically, my mouth watering at the prospect. We were informed that some goodies would be brought to us shortly. I just kept picturing that smooth pint of Guinness cradled in my hand then imagined it hitting my lips, washing over my taste buds and finally, pouring down my throat. Ah, sheer bliss!

When our BBC host had departed we lost no time in discarding our soaking wet clothes and diving straight into the warm sanctuary of our sleeping bags. We gave Louise the honour of going into the shower first as she was absolutely freezing. When my turn came I loitered for some time, dwelling on the sheer novelty of having a warm shower; soaking up the hot spray and finally feeling the warmth creep back into my knackered body. Try as I might, I could not remove all the camouflage cream from my face and even resorted at one point to rubbing it with a scrubbing brush, which wasn't very wise and had me whimpering pathetically. I'm sure they (the DS) gave us black gloss paint mixed in with the cream for a laugh, for it just seemed torturously hard to come off. It was days before I managed to cleanse my skin properly. We all looked a bit rough, especially us guys, sporting a wild, unshaven look, and were all much leaner than when we had started, but one good thing since having the showers, our body odour was now more presentable in company. We must have smelt like an elephant's armpit on a hot day in the jungle. It was a great feeling just relaxing in the bunk and reminiscing about all the things we had done over the last ten days. I honestly believed that whatever we did with the rest of our lives, no ten days would ever come near to those, which we had just completed, not by a long way! We all agreed it had been hellish good fun though.

The bunkhouse door swung open to interrupt our little talk and in stepped a girl from the BBC with a few bottles of beer and some sandwiches and biscuits. She apologised for the lack of Guinness but really, by then I was past the feeling of wanting a beer anyway. I laughed and thought about our intended night under the bridge whilst on the Escape and Evasion exercise and decided this was slightly more comfortable. The time was around 04.00am and just before we all crashed out, two unexpected visitors strolled in. It was two of the Directing Staff. They had come to wish us well for the last parade, as they had to make the journey back down South immediately. A couple of hours' sleep was all they had had and now they were about to embark on an eight hour journey! I felt very honoured and privileged to be in their company, and just being able to talk with them and share a joke or two. We all wished them a safe journey. Eventually my eyelids felt like someone had tied a pair of dumb-bells to them, while my brain shut down and dreamland beckoned.

CHAPTER 13

Day 11

"Well Done Action Man"

Wednesday 5th September 2001.

    Seven years ago on this very day, my wife gave birth to our first child, my beautiful, beautiful son Cailean. My little boy means the world to me as does my lovely wee princess Eilidh and my dear wife Sue. It is extremely hard for me to imagine how my life would have turned out if I had not met my wife, and watched as our little family unit grew into a bond of sheer friendship and love. Eleven years of marriage and we are still going as strong as day one. Anyone who trains frequently and intensively will know the need for balance in a family relationship and I am extremely grateful for my wife's understanding when it comes to matters of time aside for training. It is a huge part of my life. It is how I live my life and probably the most important ingredient, which has shaped my character and made me the person I am today. Most people have a reason for taking part in physical exercise, maybe training specifically for a sport or wanting to increase self-confidence or looks and whatever that reason is, each individual has their own motives. I too have my own reasons for starting out on the journey I undertook. The older I've got, the more I've realised that I just love pushing myself physically and mentally. I really do enjoy being up against 'it' and that 'it' could be anything from hanging in there on a sweat-drenched training session to battling through the ferocity of a mountain top blizzard in the Scottish Highlands. There is no other way to describe it. For me it's just immensely enjoyable. The desire to be competitive has never been that strong in a sporting sense. I much prefer the fight with one's own mind, and I believe this whole course was more about the mental side (you had to be mental in the first place to sign up for it!) than any other thing. Anyone can get himself or herself into good shape, but to train the brain is the ultimate workout.

As I awoke from a brief and inadequate sleep, little did I realise that today was going to be one of the greatest days of my life so far? I had managed about four-and-a-half hours' sleep but for some strange reason, felt no strong urge to rest longer. Once the eyes were opened it was time to get up. I wish I could have carried that discipline to the present, when I get up in the mornings for work in the factory. I guess jumping out of a plane or being hunted on an Escape and Evasion is a tad more exciting than the robotic monotony of an assembly line.

The first thought to enter my mind was imagining my son opening his presents in a frenzied, uncontrolled excitement. I dearly wished I could be there with him, but I also dearly loved being where I was at the moment. In any case, this would all be over in a short while. The mood between us that morning was one of slight emptiness due to the fact that we would all be going our separate ways in a few hours' time. The latter days of the programme had been very special as we built up a good rapport with one another and before we stepped out into the glorious, sunlit morning, we wished each other a final 'Good luck.' A small breakfast was served up in the farmhouse office - the very same one where we had recovered after our night of hell in interrogation. Memories came rushing back like a video recorder fast rewinding on picture search. I made up my mind there and then, that when I got back home I was racing down into town for a copy of '20 White Noise Classics', just to keep for those moments when the kids are stepping out of line.

We sat there on the soft, comfy settee, Nic, Louise, Colin and myself, lost for a moment in time, each recalling his or her own personal images and memories from the previous ten days. I think that at this point it must have dawned on us all that we had survived. We had taken everything they had thrown at us and emerged at the other side, emotionally and physically unstable and probably scarred for life. Just kidding! It was the best rollercoaster ride ever! Every emotion had played a part, at times going from extreme highs to deep lows with ecstasy, fear, trepidation and elation, all thrown in; the whole range in fact.

I swallowed the last of my coffee and wandered outside to soak up the brilliant sunshine. The four of us gathered together and lazed around while we waited on the BBC for final instructions. One of the SAS guys approached us and asked Louise to follow him. The three of us watched inquisitively as she disappeared around the corner of the farmhouse building. 'I wonder what's up,' said Nic. We just looked at each other and shrugged our shoulders, askance.

A few moments later, she reappeared and asked me to go and see the DS. 'What the hell is up?' I thought. Louise whispered very quickly that the matter of concern was, the possibility that any of us had hitched a lift or cheated during the marches. I turned the corner and was confronted by Eddie and another of the DS. 'Staff,' I acknowledged. We met eye to eye. His question was straight and to the point. 'Did you accept a lift from a vehicle during Long Drag or any of the other marches?' 'No Staff, I would never use dishonest means to pass a test,' I stated. And I wouldn't. If something was so painful and physically demanding, and it was going to take me all day or even all week, then that's what it would take, but I was damn well going to finish the particular exercise. 'Send Colin round,' said Eddie, 'and don't say a word of this.' 'Staff,' I answered, swivelling round and taking my leave. 'Colin, Eddie wants to see you.'

As Colin passed me he said 'I've blown it. I took a lift on that tractor with a few of the others during Long Drag.' All credit to the big man. He could have kept his mouth shut and denied all knowledge of any involvement, but I think DS knew anyway.

As we found out later, some of the other contestants had spilled the beans on the affair in question. Colin held his hand up like a man. When he came back he summoned Nic, who was last up. Colin could not stop beating himself up over jumping on the tractor to save a few miles on the road. It's hard to swim against the flow of opinion when everyone else in the group decides en mass, to hop on. During moments like these, one's conscience is severely tested. We offered words of support to keep Colin from getting too hung up on the situation, and who knows how the DS were selecting the final contestant.

At length, we were asked to make our way back down to camp for the final time where the closing scenes would be shot, wrapping up the whole programme. We pulled our camp beds out from the tent, stripped to the waist and sprawled out, soaking up the rays from the hot September sun. One thing we all agreed on as we chatted away, was the two Portaloos situated just outside the perimeter fence and how we were going to miss them. NOT! Imagine (well try not to) how they smelled and looked on this final day after constant bombardment from 29 bodies down to us, the last four. It was a major test in itself, enduring the unbelievable stench.

Hey, I am starting to sound soft here. SAS Are You Tough Enough? 'Well no, not really.' Not if we have to use these latrines for another week, no way.' We smartened ourselves up in preparation for the last parade. There would be no more 'On the truck' but the swarm of butterflies, which had been my constant companions and friends throughout, returned to the pit of my stomach once more in anticipation of the outcome. Eddie shouted 'Line up,' and we were over sharp, rifles by our sides, shoulders back and chin up. I think we all felt good, an immense feeling of achievement running through our blood, something no one could take from us, ever. Eddie Stone congratulated each one of us on making it to the end and gave us all a genuine feeling of pride, echoed in his sentiments. A myriad of questions and statements flew around in my head in those brief moments before he delivered his answer. 'Who is it going to be?' 'What if it's me?' 'Have I done enough?' 'What did the DS make of us?' I would be lying if I said I did not think I was in with a shout. In truth, we all were. I still thought Colin may have just shaded it over the rest of us, but maybe the tractor situation would be detrimental to his chances of being crowned 'the winner'.

On summing up his speech, Eddie emphasised how tough it had been to make a decision on who should win overall, stating earlier that the SAS guys themselves would have preferred to leave us as a final group of four. For the sake of an end result for TV, they had decided that Gary Robertson had just edged it.

'Was I hearing right?' Eddie had just mentioned my name. He came over to shake my hand and congratulate me. I was stunned. A half smile came over my face as I accepted the accolade and meekly whispered out, 'Thank you Staff!' Gobsmacked was an understatement.

I have often watched programmes on TV where someone has won something and have commented to my wife on their lack of enthusiasm saying, 'If that was me, I would be doing back flips and cartwheels.' Well now it was me who was centre stage and I decided to keep the lid on it. No hollering or giving it 'what for' and whooping it up, certainly not in front of the DS. I wanted to give them the respect they deserved and also to my fellow contestants who were also my friends. The last thing I wanted to do was prance about like a loony. For someone observing, externally, I must have looked calm and reserved, but internally my stomach felt like a food mixer on full speed. A massive rush filled my body from head to toe giving me a feeling to rival that 'Christmas morning wake-up feeling' as a child. Louise, Colin and Nic congratulated me and it made me quite emotional although I managed to hold it together. We each knew what the other had been through to get here, giving a deep feeling of mutual respect between us. I now classed these people as good friends and hoped they felt the same about me.

Dermot O'Leary conducted his final interview asking me what it meant to win and what were my thoughts and feelings on the Hell or Paradise of the last ten days. Winning had given me a very proud and special moment in my life, an accomplishment which I doubt could ever be bettered, but I feel a part of my success was down to the great friendship, camaraderie and teamwork which had bonded a bunch of total strangers like us together. Sure, we all set out from the off as solo contenders and had our own aspirations and goals set for ourselves, but the fact remains that without co-operation from each other, especially during the last three or four days, it could have been a very different story. I don't think any of the contestants I had gotten to know had a selfish attitude or an ego to try and impress. All that is good in human beings was witnessed in the sharing of food we had acquired together with the helping and encouraging each other. Great memories I will cherish forever!

I arrived on Day 1 planning to take each day as it came and see how far it got me. Apprehension niggled away inside when I heard the calibre of the people surrounding me and I suppose I was as guilty as anyone when I had seen Karl take off like a jet propelled gazelle on the hills. I pencilled him in to win the show right there and then, but on the other hand, I just thought 'Sod it, I'll keep plugging away. You never know.' I do not believe for one minute I was the fittest person among the 29 volunteers who originally started, so the question remains, how did someone like me come to end up being 'selected' by the SAS. The answer is, I don't really know. All I can say is that I had prepared for it with extreme devotion and a passion to prove to myself that I could take on my own mind and beat it, however hard the tasks became.

What did I think of the SAS? I find it hard to describe that question in words, but here goes. I was under no illusions whatsoever regarding what I had just achieved in relation to what the proper-trained candidates go through on a real Selection. We only had a very small glimpse and experience of what these guys go through on their way to being 'badged', but the public misconception of supermen in black suits and balaclavas could not have been further from the truth. They were all ordinary guys just like us, but they had been tested in probably the most rigorous, arduous and mentally taxing course in the military or civilian world. They had emerged with distinction and also I'm guessing, a greater knowledge of who they were and what they could possibly achieve in their lives. Like I said at the start, this was a dream come true for me to be involved in and I feel utterly privileged to have been a part of the set up. I can only thank the BBC and the SAS lads from the bottom of my heart for giving me a 'chance in a lifetime' opportunity to test myself and thank them also for the great fun I had along the way.

The final question I was asked by the BBC was 'Would I ever think of joining the military for real?' Maybe if I was 18 years-old again, the call of the Paras could possibly have lured me, but at the age of 34 and being happily married with a young family, I know exactly where my priorities lay, although if Eddie had said 'Do you fancy another two weeks?' I would have been at the front of the queue! We were able to chat informally with the crew when the cameras stopped rolling and they seemed very excited about the footage they had 'in the can' and the effect it may have on the public when it went out on to our screens. Way back on that first day of arrival in camp which now seemed like a lifetime ago, we had been told there would be nothing for us at the end of it. No cash prize or exotic holiday, nothing! People may call me a liar for saying this, but I was glad. It meant there would be no extra motivation channelled into our efforts in order to win a prize. We were playing from the heart. Of course I would not have said 'No' to something when the show was finished, but the feelings and learning I gained emotionally, far outweighed any pot of gold waiting at the end of the rainbow. Lots of people these days place far too much importance on material things and class you on what you have or own. I could not have been happier. Eddie, our Staff Sergeant, and at times a real bastard, came to us and shook hands warmly, while sharing a laugh and joke with us. During the course, he handled us like the professional he was and in my eyes was the perfect man for the job. He said to me 'You could have fuckin' smiled at the end, there.' I tried to splutter out an excuse and my reasoning, but what was the point. Then he added with a smile, 'It wasn't because you're a Jock either that you were picked,' referring to the fact that we were two Jocks on home territory - and on that note, he parted. What a man!

We also said goodbye to Dermot who had been a fantastic host. He was just like one of the lads, making everyone feel very relaxed on camera, which is not easy when you are talking to a star. As the camp began to get dismantled, it was time for us to collect our gear and hop into the Land Rover. I surveyed the surrounding hills as we departed camp and told myself I would have to come back in years to come for a nostalgic visit. We were to be taken for a slap-up meal at a local hotel, which quickly changed to a slap-up snack from a supermarket. Still, the food was welcome and was eaten alfresco sitting on the pavement. Apparently the BBC were in a hurry to get back down South and the hotel idea was aborted, but what the hell! We all agreed on one thing, when we got home after eleven starving days, cholesterol was on the menu, and loads of it.

I was dropped off first at Stirling Train Station and said cheerio to the guys, promising to stay in touch. Half an hour later and I was swaying gently to the rhythm of the carriage and on my way northwards and home. I sat on my holdall of unused gear and chuckled to myself. I could have brought all my Selection course needs in a carrier bag. Many people around me had just finished work and were browsing through the days' news in the papers or staring blankly into the many fields, which were hurtling by us. Just like on the first journey, I tried to imagine what they were thinking then converted to what I was thinking. 'You lucky bastard,' I told myself. I reminisced and pictured many of those trips into the hills carrying the small caravan on my back for miles and miles and assured myself it had been well worth the pain and struggle. The harsh winter conditions on a mountain-top, struggling to stay upright in the sharp teeth of a fearsome gale when the easy option was a pint of Guinness by a roaring fire in the Clachaig Inn in Glencoe. The countless miles of running, bagwork, circuit training and weights. The hard solitary training, pushing the boundaries and gritting the teeth which no one sees. All paid for in hard earned sweat for the culminate pleasure of spending '11 days in a Hell called Paradise'. 'Yes my son, be proud.' I felt no guilt at all in quietly awarding myself a little pat on the back, just this once.

Sue was waiting at Dundee Station for me and I nearly hugged her to death when we embraced. I clocked the shocked look on her face when she set eyes on me as I approached her. I had not shaven since leaving home and must have looked a little rough to say the least. Her first comment was on how thin and drawn I looked and it hit me how genuinely concerned she was for my wellbeing. The fact I still had cam cream engrained on my face did not help either. I reassured her that I felt great, probably the most physically, mentally and spiritually content that I had ever felt, but most importantly, it was damn good to be home again! Her hair smelled soothingly sweet and fresh as I nestled my weary head into her soft neck. I asked where the kids were and she told me that they were with many of our family and friends who had turned up at our home to hand in birthday presents for Cailean. My arrival home would be a timely one. I travelled home in the car in a trance-like state, my mind partially still back at camp.

'So did you win?' she nonchalantly asked, snapping me out of my temporary dream. 'I am saying nothing,' I replied and left it at that. She knew I had done well due to the fact that I was still there at the end, but I swore to myself that no one would be told the final outcome and that unfortunately, included even my wife. To be honest, it seemed really strange to be back to normality and oddly, both of us never exchanged many words as the car turned the corner and finally entered our street. I glanced towards my house to see a huge white banner draped from the bedroom window with the words 'Well Done Action Man' emblazoned across the length of it and one of my son's toy Action Man figures abseiling down the wall. A garden full of friendly and familiar faces began cheering when they spotted the car. I felt a little embarrassed; my mind was still elsewhere. When I got out of the car, I made straight for my kids and felt my eyes fill up as emotions took over. I could have put raspberry jam on them and just eaten them, there and then.

I managed to get out a 'Happy Birthday son' before I was hit with a deluge of questions from each and everyone there, all eager to know how it had gone. It would be fair to say that most of the people there were also quite shocked at the state of me, but I assured them I had never felt better. It was hard work convincing them though. In between hearing what presents my son had received for his birthday, I hugged and shook hands with them all and tried to answer as many of their questions as I could. Mum and Dad stood patiently in the background with a proud look on their faces. I gave them a massive hug as I remembered their last words before I had left which were, 'Just do your best son.' Well they would find out in good time.

Some people couldn't resist asking the direct question of 'Did you win then?' but the face of a poker player met them, expressionless and non-committing. This cat was now a 'semi-professional prisoner' who had gone through mind-numbing white noise, physically demanding stress positions and intense psychological questioning, so the chances of them breaking me were bordering on zero! The reality of it though was I wanted to get up on the rooftop and scream 'YES I DID DO IT!'

Someone asked if I was hungry at all which instantly diverted my focus away from the punishing SAS course and onto the mouth-watering thought of a chip shop meal. Ten minutes later I was devouring a greasy, fat-saturated supper like a wild beast with an eating disorder. It certainly beat the dried curry and rice from the ration pack – but not by much! When most of the well-wishers had departed, I managed to grab some quality time with my wife and kids and settle back into home life, where I watched Scotland being walloped by Belgium in a World Cup qualifier and go tumbling out of the World Cup. Some things never change…

CHAPTER 14

Life after Drumlean

In the days and weeks which followed my arrival home and the end of the biggest adventure of my life, I still found myself 'wandering' back to camp and replaying events which were still very fresh in my mind. I sat down to write a short diary of my time with the SAS, a sort of keepsake which I could re-read in years to come when I was an old bugger in a pensioner's club looking to reminisce with friends. I then had the idea of writing a full account from a contestants' perspective, and hoped to give the armchair reader or any reader for that matter a good look inside my head and an idea of what exactly made me tick. I suppose looking back now, I probably used the word 'adrenaline' on a few occasions too many, but it was the only appropriate word to describe how my body was reacting to the fear, anticipation, extreme stress and high excitement which I found myself totally submersed in.

The 'Selection' course had brought all of the aforementioned feelings and more in abundance, and not just on some days - it was every day. The broad view of an 'adrenaline junkie' is someone who takes unnecessary risks and has a death wish, someone who is willing themselves to die whilst in the process of doing something considered to be highly dangerous. I prefer to go along with the exact opposite opinion. It is a supreme life wish. It is all about risk and how far we should push our boundaries. They say, from the second we enter into this world we are taking a risk. Life quite literally is full of danger and comes in many different forms but living a life cocooned in a cotton wool-wrapped comfort zone will not save us from our fate. In my own view, if we are sensible enough and not stupid about taking risks then the opportunities are out there to be grabbed with open arms. Saying 'I can't' can be pushed from our thoughts with the encouragement, belief and positive guidance from others. It's true - anyone and everyone CAN!

For me personally, the parachute jump was the ultimate 'high' and I think the same went for everyone else who was left on the programme at that stage although collectively, everything was a high. I went back to the

Skydiving Club in St Andrews, only a month after being there with the BBC and did another fixed-line jump from 3,500feet. My dad, Sue and the kids accompanied me to lend their support and it was much appreciated, as the feelings of dread and excitement were exactly the same as the first time. Once I had made the phone call and received confirmation that I would be jumping, I instantly thought, 'What the hell are you thinking about, you don't need to go and do this. You've already proved you've got the bottle.' If I'm honest with myself, I would probably say that the reason to go and jump again was to prove that I could do it a second time. The plane I boarded was twin-engined, bigger in size than the previous one and full of other jumpers who were mainly freefallers. Conditions were fairly cramped as I squeezed onto the last available space on the floor. Being last man on meant I was first man out and I remained calm all the way during the climb to the designated height, but when the jump master slid the door open, I looked down and thought 'What the fuck am I doing here?'

The pilot banked the plane over in order to line up with the DZ (drop zone), at which point I nearly shit myself. Another distraction apart from the void between the planet and me was a large rudder type panel hanging down from the engine on the wing, which was situated only five or six feet from the doorway. I had the awful feeling when I pushed myself off that I was going to slam into it, which was nigh on impossible considering the little matter of air and the velocity it was flying by at. Approximately ten seconds later, I was comfortably dangling above the Earth admiring the view and feeling hugely relieved that the large silk tablecloth above my head was still holding my weight.

Three days rest was the treat I had given to myself on completion of the course, and then it was back to the business of training as usual. The call of the mountains was and still is never far away and I was back scaling a few peaks way up in the North West of Scotland in a majestic little place called Torridon, only two weeks or so after the programme's finale. It felt good to be out with the lads again laughing in the face of atrocious weather conditions whilst desperately trying to erect our tents in the dismal, gloomy darkness, although the visit to the local inn prior, definitely helped keep our spirits high. Morning saw conditions take a turn for the worse (if that was at all possible!) and pessimistic remarks started flying around the minibus on route to the starting point of our chosen foray. A few of the squad never even ventured out of their sleeping bags until midday when their hunger pangs told them to go and have a well-earned bar lunch. What happened to the tough men of the mountains? Leaving the warmth of the minibus and stepping out into the harsh gale and torrential rain was a major test on the willpower. Only the very lowest parts of the mountains were visible and everywhere the sight of what would usually be tumbling little streams could now be classed as serious-to-cross, frothing white rapids. Most of the group turned back after a few hundred yards and never really gave the mountains a chance. George, Ronnie and myself were all that was left so now it was time to grit the teeth, get the head down and prepare for a long hard battle with the elements. And what a battle it was!

I had that awful feeling momentarily, that I was going to be seriously injured or killed when I slipped off a crag not far from the first summit. It was like a scene from a Tom and Jerry cartoon when the cat is falling and his nails are the only things that are left trying to save him. That surge of adrenaline when you know in a split second that you are about to fall is a frightening experience. Luckily I escaped with a few scrapes and bangs and went right back up it again, my whole body shaking from what had just happened. Afterwards, we were rewarded for our tenacity in braving the earlier conditions with a blue sky peppered with brilliant white, wispy clouds and a glaring sun which struck out across a little loch, situated far below us. This is where I feel the will is forged, high in the hills and mountains where digging deep inside your soul finds the strengths you never knew you had. Where the firm hand of Mother Nature can turn a pleasant day into a real battle, sometimes in extreme cases, one for survival. But the rewards are gratifying and beauty is witnessed on a grand scale, views which would rival the very best in the world. Inner peace and content are the free gifts given for effort, not forgetting the bloody good laughs along the way.

The infamous 'Tough Guy' challenge was something that had been on my list of must do's after reading about it in a magazine article some time ago. When I spoke to contestants on the SAS programme, I found out that a good few of them had taken part in Tough Guy and hearing first hand reports of its gruelling content only confirmed my willingness to enter. It is absolutely bonkers which is why I would recommend it to anyone. Basically, it consists of an eight-mile cross-country run, through knee-deep mud, pools of shitty water, uphill climbs and finally onto an assault-type course, definitely not built for the faint-hearted. As the winter event is run in January and a fair amount of the course involves submersing yourself under the water, temperatures make for interesting play when your head goes under, giving you one of the worst sensations on the brain imaginable. It is a real test of courage and endurance taken up by both males and females of all ages, shapes and sizes and is competitively fought out in the good name of charity.

Some of us kept in touch after the programme's completion and even teamed up for a few events, keeping up the great camaraderie which we enjoyed during filming. Between us all as contestants, there was a real mixture of interests and by keeping in touch, new opportunities presented themselves, being only a phone call or email away.

And so, the anxious wait to see the whole thing screened on television ate into my patience. Originally, the programme had been scheduled to go out in November 2001 but the horrendous acts of terrorism on September 11th ultimately delayed the screening for obvious reasons. It would have been highly insensitive of the BBC to allow a 'reality programme' airtime when real SAS guys might be involved in a war situation. SAS: Are you tough enough? eventually found a slot on a Sunday evening in March 2002 and ran for three weeks, an hour at a time. I must admit, my excitement was at exploding point in the lead-up to the first episode being shown. I remember one evening whilst making a sandwich in the kitchen, Sue let out a hellish scream and came running through at breakneck speed to tell me I was on TV in a preview for the programme. It really was a strange feeling to see your face on national TV; after all I was just that guy called Joe Bloggs from down the street. Incidentally, I had managed to keep the end result and general happenings of the programme hush-hush, even from close family and friends for a good few months with the one exception being my wife. Literally, the cat escaped from the bag right at the start when she deviously extracted the answer from me after telling a small lie and saying that she had heard a conversation over the phone between Cass and myself concerning the show. Only a few weeks earlier, I had managed to get through some SAS interrogation and here I was tripping at the first sign of questioning from a smart little lady! I could have kicked myself. I managed to keep quiet for a while before a book was released under the same title as the programme, which gave the final outcome and so forced me into revealing the result to those closest to me. This quickly filtered through to friends and workmates, many of whom commented, 'I knew it.' They didn't know and certainly wouldn't have if the untimely launch of the book was held back until after the final episode. Most people were genuinely interested in how the challenge had gone, but a few only seemed eager to know what prize I had won. Their empty minds would never understand.

The levels of excitement and anticipation grew to fever pitch as I sat with my wife Sue and children Cailean and Eilidh to watch the first instalment of SAS: Are you tough enough? I constantly kept butting in and explaining in greater detail the finer points of what we were actually doing or going through, all to the complete annoyance of my family. The one-hour episode seemed to be over in five minutes and had us asking for more. After the final credits rolled up, our phone began ringing fairly regularly with well-wishers saying how much they had enjoyed it and couldn't wait till next weeks' showing. When I went to work on Monday morning, colleagues bombarded me with questions and some people I never even knew, approached to congratulate and question me on many wide and varied aspects of the show.

The following Sunday was much the same as the previous one with lots of interest being generated locally. For the approach of the final episode I was away for most of the weekend down in Wales and in my absence, Sue and the rest of the family had taken the time and effort to organize a surprise party for me in a local bar. I suspected something was going on when the taxi pulled up outside the front door but I honestly thought I would only be meeting my family and some close friends. Disbelief was the most apt way to describe my feelings as I opened the swing doors and walked into the function suite. Everywhere I looked, a familiar face smiled back at me. It seemed that just about everyone who knew me was in the place to watch the final drama on a huge screen. Funnily enough whilst watching my efforts in the swimming pool, I found myself, along with everyone else, holding my breath for the final breadth underwater. It was a strange feeling, especially as I already knew I would make it to the other side! It was one of the best and most memorable nights of my life and went on into the early hours of the morning. Thankfully, I was on a nightshift and able to sleep off the celebratory effects of a 'few too many'.

The aftermath of it all was a thoroughly enjoyable experience. Like I mentioned earlier strangers introduced themselves and wanted to know how I had felt physically and mentally during the whole process. Among some of the 'perks' of winning the show was an invite to a local

Sportsman's Dinner and being a guest of honour at the opening of a Fitness Studio in Kendal along with Colin from the programme.

I find it slightly amusing to witness some of the contestants from the many other Reality TV shows now flooding our screens, being given star-status and bringing out fitness videos and DVD's amongst other things. Good luck to them all and their success but I will always be content in the knowledge that we (contestants) as a whole, were involved in the toughest show of them all without question, and I'm just happy to have been given the opportunity to give it a try.

So, would I do it all again? The sixty pounds of unused gear would be packed into that holdall so fast I would be on location before the phone was put down. The answer is an emphatic YES!

Since I began writing this story, SAS: Jungle are you tough enough? has been and gone and right now as I type, the last episode has just finished for the third series called SAS: Desert are you tough enough? The jungle series was filmed in Borneo and looked incredibly tough with the conditions alone being a major cause for concern. Two females made it to the last four and the final choice must have been a very hard decision to make as they had all performed equally well. In the end the DS ultimately chose one of the females named Gill. She must have felt absolutely elated at winning the show. In my view, the hardest series so far has been the one which has just finished in the Namibian desert, although dealing with the 100-degree heat has looked nothing compared to dealing with the intimidating figure of Staff Sergeant Eddie Stone. He really is a genuinely scary bloke and I found myself cringing for the contestants when they messed something up or tried answering him back. Two females again managed to make it to the last four when many of the stronger-seeming male characters folded. It just proves that some women can match the men physically and certainly mentally when it comes to testing the human body in a severe environment.

Will there be any more series? I would like to think yes. One thing is for certain, the whole concept of being tested by the SAS and showing it to the general public has proved to be hugely popular and the best bit about it is that there is no fame and fortune at the end of it all. We all just simply drift back into our daily business.

Epilogue

The trees laid bare for the season of winter silently bend their branches to the forceful command of an angry wind. Sparrows and starlings battle to keep a course as they fly around on a daily forage for food. She views this picture of life from the warm confines of a homely conservatory and smiles. Always she smiles, and hopes.

Her last session of chemotherapy for the time being has passed and with it, an anxious, mind-numbing wait for her results. Her fears and worries are buried behind a brave mask of happiness for us all. My mother-in-law, Margaret Macdonald's on-going battle with cancer continues. Her sheer courage and tenacity, her ability to always smile, even when the pain is biting hard is an immense inspiration to all the family.

Mum, you are a fighter and the epitome of what 'real tough' is.

We love you always.

Fancy having a go at some similar type challenges, or maybe something just a little less strenuous with a lighter, more fun-feel to it? At Tactical Control Group (situated near Aberfoyle in Stirlingshire, Scotland,) ex-SAS Staff Sergeant Eddie Stone and his team of highly professional associates can provide various challenges to suit your needs.

Check out the fantastic website for more details.

www.tacticalcontrolgroup.com